Moments to Hold Close

Moments to Hold Close

Mouzon Biggs, Jr.

ABINGDON PRESS
Nashville

MOMENTS TO HOLD CLOSE

Copyright © 1983 by Abingdon Press

All Rights Reserved
No part of this book may be reproduced in any manner
whatsoever without written permission of the publisher
except brief quotations embodied in critical articles
or reviews. For information address Abingdon Press,
Nashville, Tennessee.

Library of Congress Cataloging in Publication Data

Biggs, Mouzon.
  Moments to hold close.
  1. Meditations. 2. Biggs, Mouzon. I. Title.
BV 4832.2.B49 1983   242   82-16446

ISBN 0-687-27147-9

MANUFACTURED BY THE PARTHENON PRESS AT
NASHVILLE, TENNESSEE, UNITED STATES OF AMERICA

This book is dedicated to my mother and father, Tula and Mouzon Biggs, who first taught me to see the special in the everyday.

CONTENTS

FOREWORD

After Mouzon Biggs, Jr. was appointed pastor of Boston Avenue Church in Tulsa, he and a friend were discussing the task before him. The friend pointed out that he was going to one of the most distinguished pulpits in The United Methodist Church.

The friend named five ministers who had most recently served that great church—John W. Russell, J. Chess Lovern, Finis A. Crutchfield, Paul V. Galloway, Bascom Watts—each of whom was elected a bishop and each of whom is unusually respected. Then the friend asked, "Do you think you can live up to the standards those men set?"

With his characteristic smile, in a low-key voice, Mouzon Biggs simply replied, "All I will be concerned about is that every day I give my very best."

The giving of his very best and not worrying about somebody else has been the motivating philosophy of Mouzon Biggs. And that has been enough in every position he has held.

While a student at Centenary College and the Perkins School of Theology of Southern Methodist University, he served as pastor of Mt. Zion Church, a small rural church. Today, people in the church talk about the outstanding ministry of Mouzon Biggs. The same is true at the three other places he has served. He was one of the ministers at Memorial Drive and First Church in Houston, and senior minister at Trinity United Methodist Church in Beaumont. Each of these churches love and appreciate him and his lovely wife, Gayle.

In *Moments to Hold Close*, one sees some of the deep insights of Mouzon Biggs. He not only is a genuine scholar, he has an understanding and genuine concern for people. Reading these insights, one finds help and encouragement for one's own living. I personally felt inspired and helped as I shared with Dr. Biggs, through these pages, his own life experiences.

A personal word—Mouzon Biggs and I worked together for seven years on the staff of First United Methodist Church in Houston. I have never known a more effective minister than he. His friendship has warmed my heart and blessed my life. He is truly one of the most respected ministers in our country.

Charles L. Allen

PREFACE

Shortly before I left Beaumont, Texas, to become pastor of Tulsa's Boston Avenue Church, Lamar University hired a new head football coach. Coach Larry Kennan brought enthusiasm and energy to a team that had lost ten games the year before. His first ballgame that year was against Southwest Conference champion Baylor University. Lamar's Cardinals fought Baylor all the way, but were beaten in the fourth quarter.

A television reporter met Coach Kennan at the dressing room door and asked, "Well, coach, this has to be a downer for you and your team, doesn't it? I mean, after playing at such a high emotional level, losing has to be a real downer. Old nightmares come again."

Calmly Coach Kennan replied, "We are a new team

with a new direction. There will be no downers for this team. We will learn from every experience."

On a different level Paul was trying to convey the same attitude to the Christians at Rome, "Let us even exult in our present sufferings, because we know that suffering trains us to endure, and endurance brings proof that we have stood the test, and this proof is the ground of hope" (Romans 5:3-4 NEB).

Paul continued, "And we know that all things work together for good to them that love God, to them who are the called according to his purpose." (Romans 8:28)

Christians have the same hurts, frustrations, hopes, and dreams as non-Christians. But if they walk with Christ, they learn to hold close some moments and cleanse their minds of others.

I have recorded here some moments I continue to hold close. Every hand's a winner, if you know what to hold and what to throw away.

Mouzon Biggs, Jr.
Boston Avenue United Methodist Church

"I Know How to Be One Now"

Luke 10:25-37
"But he . . . said to Jesus, 'And who is my neighbor?' " (v. 29 RSV)

That little light kept blinking, on-off-on-off. I knew somebody must be waiting on that other telephone line, but I was talking to a church member about the funeral for her brother. The other caller would have to wait, even though my secretary had buzzed me twice.

Ten minutes later, funeral arrangements having been finalized, I answered the other line, "Hello."

"Mouzon? Ralph, Ralph Wyler. I'm calling from Washington state."

My mind flipped back ten years. Ralph was a

13

member of a church in Houston. He had just gone through a very unhappy divorce. His wife said she still loved him, but she just could not deal with his alcoholism. She asked for custody of their young sons. It was granted.

Ralph had gotten worse in his disease. He tried a rebound marriage. She was a very pretty woman, but she brought as many problems to the marriage as Ralph did. She had a teen-age daughter who was running with a fast crowd of drug-users. The marriage failed.

Ralph had the shakes almost all the time. He thought it was nerves. His friends thought it was his drinking. Four years later it would be diagnosed as Parkinson's disease.

One year, a few days before Christmas, Ralph had ended up in a halfway house for alcoholics. The director of the house called me late that afternoon. It was time for me to go home. Rush hour traffic was heavy by that time. I lived four miles west of the church. The halfway house was three miles south and east. It would take almost two extra hours to go and see Ralph, but I told the director I would be there as soon as I could drive through the downtown holiday traffic.

With a drunken slur Ralph had greeted me, "Mouzon, I'm so glad you came. How about loaning me two dollars to buy some cigarettes?"

"The director provides free cigarettes," I answered.

"Well, I need money to call my kids."

"The director will let you use the phone free as soon as you dry out."

"So you aren't going to help me! You don't really care!" His voice grew louder and louder. Other men gathered around. "You preach it, but you don't live it. You don't really care."

I waited for him to wind down. Then I spoke calmly, "Ralph, I am willing to do one thing for you. I will be your friend."

"Good," he answered. "Two dollars will be fine."

"No money this time," I responded. "Just friendship. I want to be your friend, but I get to decide what it means for me to be your friend. And you have to decide what it means to be mine."

It was that Ralph on the phone. "Washington? Ralph, how are you?"

"Mouzon, I have a good illustration for your Christmas sermon—me. I lost everything after you left Houston. I ran. The farthest place I could find from Houston was Washington. I have Parkinson's, but in my mind and heart, I am getting well. I have not had a drink in three years. I have a small private business here, and I am feeling so much better about myself. Last Sunday at the church, I decided to call you just before Christmas Day."

"Well, I am so glad you did. I can always use a great Christmas story."

"Mouzon," he asked slowly, "one more question— could you use one more friend? I think I know how to be one now."

"In the Corner of That Fence"

John 4:7-26
"Our fathers worshiped on this mountain." (v. 20 RSV)

"I'll bet you get tired of visiting me," he sighed. "I know I get tired of being sick."

He pulled himself up higher in the bed. "The longer I'm sick, the more important some questions become," he said. "I have two tough ones for you today."

I nodded my head to show my willingness to help. He did not seem to need much encouragement.

"When I was a boy, I remember preachers getting all worked up about an unpardonable sin. They used to scare me. Maybe I was so scared because I never did understand what they were saying." He chuckled a little as he and I both pictured the old brush arbors and sawdust revivals.

But his smile faded. His eyes became more intent. "That unpardonable sin had something to do with the Holy Spirit, didn't it?"

"You and I probably heard some of the same sermons," I answered. "Blasphemy against the Holy Spirit was usually their theme."

"Right," he broke in. "What does blasphemy mean?"

"Blasphemy is a word describing slander against

God or God's actions. Some persons accused Jesus of blasphemy against God because they believed only God could forgive sin. They were not willing to believe that God was in Christ."

He leaned forward a little, hanging on my words. I was afraid my language was not very helpful. Church talk sounds impressive but may not answer our questions in words that we really understand.

But I charged ahead anyway. "Blasphemy against the Holy Spirit was seen as a deliberate denial of God's work whereby one consciously hardens himself against repentance and the possibility of forgiveness." Having poured out that long sentence, I felt confident that I had given the church's established definition. I was not so sure that the words meant so much to my friend.

His eyes still showed some confusion, so I tried again, "In other words, if you are still concerned about how God feels about you, if you are willing to give him credit for all that is good and beautiful and true, if you are willing to let him love you, then you do not have to be afraid of an unforgiveable sin."

His eyes welled with tears. One spilled out and followed the soft wrinkles around his eyes. "I care," he said softly.

Then his eyes brightened and cleared, "One more for today."

"Fine. Shoot," I responded.

"When I was a boy, we all lived on a farm. We worked hard. We worked long hours in the hot sun. But my mama and daddy kept us close to God and close to each other."

He paused to take a sip of water and glanced around to acknowledge a nurse at the door. When she left, he went on, "I had a special place to pray. Nobody told me to pray there. It just looked like a good place. It was private and quiet. You know how folks used to make rail fences that zigzagged over the hills? Well, down below our house near the creek, I found a corner of an old rail fence. I was about twelve or thirteen, tired of being a boy, afraid I would never be a man. I knelt down in that corner and prayed. I felt that God was awful close."

His voice quivered a moment. These memories were very old and very special. "I prayed there once or twice a week, till I was grown and married!"

He swallowed hard, "Do you think God would make me well if I could kneel again in the corner of that fence?"

Who Profits Most?

Luke 9:18-27
"Whoever loses his life for my sake, he will save it." (v. 24 RSV)

"How do you keep yourself under control when you have only one ski?" I asked.

He chuckled and answered, "Somebody taught you to snowplow, right?"

I nodded.

"And it takes two skis toe-to-toe to make a plow, right?"

I nodded again.

"Well, I have my brakes on the end of my crutches." He held up a crutch, the light, tubular aluminum kind. It had the front end of a ski mounted on it. The short ski was only twelve inches long and had a serrated edge on the back end. It was easy to see how a skier could pull back on two crutches, dig those sharp edges into the snow, and slow one's speed of descent as desired.

"If you have a minute, I would love to show you some movies of our group," John said.

The projector whirred. "That's Robert. He is an amputee like I am. Watch how he negotiates that turn. Wow, Robert is so good. Now, here I come. Watch out! Man, I almost collided with the photographer. I

19

have been skiing only three times so far. I guess you are a good skier, Dr. Biggs."

"Hardly. I live so far from a mountain, I get to go skiing only once a year. How did you get started?"

"You see that guy in the next booth? This club project was his idea. One weekend he was skiing at our nearest slope. When he stopped at the bottom of the slope for a hamburger, he noticed a fellow sitting by a window. He was gazing up at the beginner's run where a woman was wrestling two small kids through the turns. The three of them finally got to the bottom. The man rose to meet them. As the man walked across the chalet dining room to reach his family, Robert noticed that he had one leg and one prosthesis. He watched them laughing and talking. When the woman and children zipped up their coats and went outside again, the man took his seat beside the window to watch. Robert walked over to the man and introduced himself. I was that man. He asked me if I would like to learn how to ski with my family."

John paused, looked again at his new friend, and then went on, "You see, Robert has only one leg, too. But mutual hardship is not the key to his wanting to help. He helps cerebral palsy kids and muscular dystrophy patients, too. Now he and I are helping two blind guys learn how to ski."

"Blind?" I asked. "How do you get a blind person down a mountain on skis?"

"Robert figured it out. We use two methods. One way is for the blind skier to visualize a clock face. Then we ski close behind and warn of a tree at eleven o'clock and forty feet or a fallen skier at one o'clock and thirty feet. The other way is to put small bells on the instructor's boots and lead the blind skier."

"Man, I can only imagine the confidence you would have to have in your instructor to follow him down a mountain you can't even see."

"Yeah, but our instructor works free, and he asks nothing in return. He is a friend. But notice that small pin he wears in his lapel. I think it tells the story."

I noticed. It had a familiar ring; "He profits most who serves best."

It could have said, "And he who loses his life shall surely find it."

When Now Is Best of All

Luke 18:9-17
"Whoever does not receive the kingdom of God like a child shall not enter it." (v. 17 RSV)

German names abound in many settlements in South Texas. I met a very interesting couple once in Yoakum, Texas, who carried the name of Riemenschneider.

The pastor of the First United Methodist Church in Yoakum had invited me to preach three days in his church. Neither I nor my wife Gayle had ever been to Yoakum, so we decided to make this a family trip.

Our children saw a lot of interesting things there. We had a tour of a leather goods plant. Our host explained the art of making saddles, from the saddle tree to buck-stitching. There were thousands of wallets and beautiful purses, bull whips, and belts.

On our third day in Yoakum we were invited to have lunch at the Riemenschneider home. The food was excellent, but the conversation was even better. For several decades this family had run a dry goods store in the main business district of this beautiful little city. One son had felt called to be a missionary, had prepared himself in college and seminary, and was teaching in a seminary in the Far East. The other son was a policeman in Harris County, Pasadena, Texas. These folks loved to talk about their past when the children were young, when their parents and grandparents talked about the "old country," when *Sauerbraten* and *Kartoffeln* filled their plates.

They also liked to talk about the future, expected visits with their sons and grandchildren.

But I was most impressed with the way they talked about their present. Mr. Riemenschneider led us to a workshop behind the main house. For a number of years his hobby had been woodwork and cabinetry. Family gifts at Christmas and birthdays were often new pieces of equipment for his shop, a lathe, drill press, or jigsaw. Now he was retired from the dry goods business and could pursue his hobby with full enthusiasm.

He showed us a beautiful wooden rocking horse. He had seen it one day beside the trash pile at the

Lutheran Church. It was worn and peeling after many years of service in the church nursery. One rocker was broken. Repairs would cost more than a new horse. But Mr. Riemenschneider enjoyed making old things become new again. He carried the horse to his shop, sanded it, built a new matching rocker, and painted it pretty and bright. It would be back in the Lutheran nursery the next Sunday, no charge to the children who would enjoy it.

A second project was for a Brownie group, girls who lived in Yoakum's poorer section. He had built doll furniture for each girl. The little dressers had real mirrors on them, drawers that opened and closed—no charge to those little girls who would enjoy them for hours and hours.

The third current project was bird feeders for Cub Scouts. He took one from the shelf and held it out to my children, "Ask your father to hang this feeder outside the window nearest your breakfast table. Buy sunflower seed and put them in the feeder, then watch the cardinals and blue jays fly in to enjoy that good food."

My children's eyes lit up as they took the feeder with green roof and glass walls from his hands. But the brightest eyes belonged to the Riemenschneiders, who enjoyed taking the old and making it new, giving to those who could guarantee no return.

The Rainbow Tunnel

Romans 8:18-39
"In everything God works for good." (v. 28 RSV)

That trip through the rainbow tunnel tied us together. The rainbow tunnel was built to join the old Hermann Hospital to the new one.

The older building had been a show place in its earlier years. It was Spanish decor and design from roof to basement. Even the stairways had arched doorways and ceilings. The Spanish tiled walls were colorful and spotless. But the years had come and gone, and the older building was inferior to the new hospitals going up in the Houston Medical Center. The open stairways were a fire hazard. The high ceilings meant more dollars for heating and cooling. A new hospital was designed and built.

Now there were two Hermann Hospital buildings. The newest and best diagnostic machines were placed in the newer building. But patients in both buildings deserved the best. So someone hit on a clever idea—connect the two buildings by tunnel. Patients could be carried by wheelchair or stretcher without leaving the controlled environment of hospital cleanliness—no problems with rain, wind, or temperature. However, there was one problem. Each building was huge. It is frightening to surrender one's clothes and crawl into any hospital bed. It was worse to be in a

24

hospital with many floors and more than a thousand beds. But, imagine trying to follow a husband, a wife, or child from one building that size into another building, through a long, crooked tunnel.

It was time for another clever idea. How about coding medical groups by color? Maternity could be pink or blue, urology could be green, cardiology could be purple, hematology could be red, and so on. If you were having blood work done in the old building, you might be asked to follow the red stripe on the floor to the hematology department in the new building. When you started down the hall, you followed a red line on the floor. At the corner, a green line joined your red one. You had just passed the urology department. Fifty feet down the hallway, a yellow line came out of a lab and joined the green and red.

All lines came together at the entrance to the tunnel. All separated at the exit from the tunnel. But inside the tunnel—a rainbow of colors on the walls and floor. It was beautiful.

Ralph Bluze was very ill. He was admitted to the older Hermann building. Every day he made a trip through the tunnel. Sometimes he followed the yellow line, sometimes the green, then the red, his family tagging along behind the wheelchair.

After a week of testing, the doctors recommended surgery. It was listed as "exploratory," but they seemed pretty confident what they would find. It looked bad. That morning before surgery, Ralph and I joined hands with Sue and the three kids for prayer, and then Ralph went through that rainbow tunnel for the last time. Whenever I preach near Houston, I can expect Sue and her children, now grown, to be on the front row.

At each end of the tunnel there were so many people, wheelchairs, corridors, glucose, bottles, and worried faces—but you could make it if you never forgot which color you were following.

Will I Be His Brother?

Genesis 4:1-9
"Am I my brother's keeper?" (v. 9 RSV)

"I just got word late last night that my wife's dying, Reverend. Any chance you could help me get home?" My early morning visitor twisted the old baseball cap he held in his hands.

"Where is home?"

"Near Little Rock, Arkansas. We live out in the country about eighteen miles from Little Rock. It must be about four hundred miles from here."

"How did you get down here on the Gulf Coast?"

"I hitchhiked. I guess you are thinking I am a little old to be running around the country. Maybe I am. But all the work dried up in Arkansas. I kept hearing about all this work in Texas. Folks told me that all the construction companies were hiring. But I have been here nearly three weeks without work. The unions were full. The day laborers had some work, but it was given to folks from Texas. I sat there in that labor pool day after day, but nobody would hire me."

"Could we call your home and see how your wife is doing this morning? Which hospital is she in?"

"She ain't in no hospital. She's at home. And we don't have a phone. My neighbors called."

"Why didn't somebody take her to a hospital?"

"Well, she wanted to go home to die. I knew she was bad off, but I had no idea she was this bad."

"Could we call the neighbors?" I asked.

"Nah, sir, that won't help. They live four miles away. If they are at home, they won't know anything new. If they know anything new it's because they are with my wife. And we don't have a phone. I just need to get home."

I called the bus station. They had a bus leaving for Little Rock in twenty-seven minutes. We were only three blocks away. I asked them to hold one seat.

"Reverend, could you allow me a little money for a cup of coffee and a doughnut? I haven't had a bite to eat in nearly two days."

I called a diner across the street from the church, "Can you fix me two hamburgers, a package of potato chips, and a cup of black coffee to go? I'll be there in ten minutes."

"Reverend, you never will regret this. If you will give me your name and address, I'll be sure to send your money back," he added.

I handed him one of my cards. We walked across the street and picked up his hamburgers and coffee. I walked with him to the bus station, bought his ticket, and shook his hand, "I will be praying for a safe trip and good news when you reach your wife."

He squeezed my hand again, "Reverend, I will never forget you." The bus rolled away.

That was five years ago. I never received a dollar, not even a card of thanks. Was his wife really sick? Did he just want a ride home?

Those questions are not my problem. My problem was not whether he would be my brother. My only question was whether I would be his.

Even When You're Losing

Psalm 63:1-4
"Because thy steadfast love is better than life, my lips will praise thee." (v. 3 RSV)

Baseball season gradually yields to football season. Then comes basketball, hockey, and track. Tennis and golf are with us always.

Any sports contest reminds us that somebody wins and somebody loses. For several years in Houston, the Touchdown Club invited me to give the opening prayer for one of its fall meetings. One year I was asked to pray at the meeting immediately preceding the Texas University versus Texas A. & M. University football game.

In past years their Thanksgiving Day game had much to do with the championship of the Southwest Conference. The alumni of both schools take this game very seriously, though the Texas University team has won most of the games in the past fifteen years.

I really agonized over my prayer. I knew that the head coaches of both schools would be addressing more than twelve hundred graduates of the two schools. The following day somebody would win, and somebody would lose.

My prayer on that occasion included the lines, "Father, all of us know how much happier we are when we win. All of us know how we hurt when we lose. Help us to help make winners of as many as we can. Help us always to stand close to those who lose."

When I concluded my prayer, I went back to my seat at one end of the head table. Coach Darrel Royal got up from his chair and came down to my end of the table. He said, "I've been going to sports banquets for more than thirty years, and I've heard a lot of invocations, but that prayer spoke to me. Could I have a copy before we leave today?"

As he returned to his chair, a sports writer for the *Houston Post* leaned over to me and said, "That Darrell Royal will do anything for a little public relations."

I said, "How is that? It was a good prayer."

"Yeah, I know, but what does Royal know about losing? He wins all the time."

"Wait a second," I replied. "I read in your paper just

a few weeks ago that Coach Royal's daughter was killed in an auto accident. Even he knows how to lose."

Some days we win. Some days we lose. But our God reminds us that he loves us every day. He wants every child of his to be a winner, but he always stays close to those who hurt. He demands that we do the same for the one standing closest to us at any moment of our lives. And when we do, both of us win. He promised.

"Tell Me Again"

Matthew 7:21-27
"Every one then who hears these words of mine and does them . . ." (v. 24 RSV)

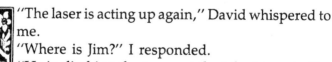"The laser is acting up again," David whispered to me.

"Where is Jim?" I responded.

"He is climbing the tower at the television studio. He has already climbed our tower twice, but he has not located the problem."

The laser had once seemed like a great idea. It was $10,000 less than a microwave unit. It was environmentally clean and completely safe. All sound and color pictures would be carried in a beam of light from our church to the television station a half mile away.

After two months of struggling to make it work, we had decided to spend the extra money for microwave units. The laser just was not working satisfactorily. Our cameras were producing brilliant color, but the television station was not receiving that same quality.

We were told that we could have a microwave system installed within a month. Now two more months had passed, and we were still limping along with an inadequate laser. But today, we had no signal at all.

Time came for the broadcast, but there would be none today. Our District Superintendent delivered a powerful sermon, our musicians sang beautifully, and our church was filled with worshipers. But no one at home could see or hear. The laser had failed again.

"It could be the transmitter or the receiver," Jim had said. "If either one fails, there is no communication."

I remembered a fall episode of "All in the Family." Archie Bunker and his wife, Edith, were having trouble. In complete frustration, Archie had shouted, "Our problem, Edith, is that I talk in English, and you hear in Dingbat."

If one is transmitting on Channel Ten, the receiver must be turned to Channel Ten. Our laser was transmitting in vivid color. But the receiver on the station tower had a bad connection. It was receiving Dingbat.

Two days before, a wife had been telling me about her family's trip home for Christmas. "Everytime we go home for a holiday, Roy makes my life miserable. He talks to me as if I were a dog."

"Have you told him how you feel?"

"At least a hundred times."

"Tell him again."

She told him. He did not really hear. He felt threatened. She was transmitting, but he was not receiving.

"Tell him again. Use different words."

She tried. He listened. He heard a little more that time.

"Say it again. Use different words," I insisted.

She started to cry. He took hold of her hand and began to stroke her fingers. His voice broke a little, but he whispered, "Tell me again. I do want to hear. Use different words."

"How Can I Trust You?"

Psalm 4:1-8
"Trust in the Lord." (v.5 RSV)

 "Do you think you are ready for a longer ride today?" I asked our Jason.

"Yes sir," he answered. Then he added, "How long do you mean?"

"About ten miles, I guess, round trip."

"I rode to the church and back," he boasted.

"Right, but that was less than four miles. Parkdale Mall is five miles from our house and five miles home."

Jason is only six. He got his first bicycle for Christmas a few weeks ago, and Gayle and I have been teaching him to ride on city streets.

A couple of Saturdays before, he and I had ridden all the way to Trinity Church and back. He loved it. He wanted to try a trip to the mall. Gayle and Trey signed on to go with us.

It was a beautiful Saturday, cool and clear. Now Jason remembered our usual route to the mall—down North Circuit to Edson, left to Gladys, right to West Lucas, left to the freeway, left to Crow Road. That is a quick, easy way in a car. But I decided to take less crowded streets on the bikes. After two unfamiliar turns, Jason was lost.

"Dad, how much farther?" he asked.

"We have gone only one mile. Are you tired?"

"No, sir. Do we turn here?"

"We will turn left at the next corner." We turned. "Slow down a little and the light will turn green for us." His legs are a little short and stopping is tough. Getting started again is even tougher. He slowed down.

"Dad?" he asked.

"Yes?"

"Are we lost?"

"No, we are almost halfway now. Are you tired?"

He assured me that he was fine. Gayle and Trey were right behind. He got quiet but kept pedaling.

"Dad, do you know the way home?"

"Sure, are you tired?"

"No, sir, but I want to be sure we can get home."

I assured him that I knew the way. I cautioned him about stop signs, fast cars, careless drivers, holes in the pavement, and bad dogs.

He pedaled along. I tried to help him think about our destination. "Hey who votes for a good cold drink at the mall? And maybe a candy bar for a little energy?"

Gayle and Trey voted yes right away, but Jason had a concerned look on his face. At every turn I could tell that he was still looking for a familiar landmark.

We slowed down for another intersection. He spoke again. "Dad?"

"Yeah, pal."

"If you get me lost this time, how am I ever going to trust you again?"

I smiled at him as we rounded the corner, and he saw the flags flying over the mall.

"May I Give Myself Again?"

Psalm 51:1-17
"A broken and contrite heart, O God, thou wilt not despise." (v. 17 RSV)

 It began as a standard gathering to honor a man who was retiring. He was scrubbed and shining. His wife wore an orchid corsage on her left shoulder. Their two children and three grandchildren were lined up across the front row of the hotel ballroom.

Everyone always looks a little uncomfortable at retirement parties. Something meaningful needs to be said. I mean, forty-seven years of work should merit some serious consideration. But emotions lie close to the surface, alongside a desire to push aside our deepest questions about life and meaning and family and friends. Any effort at humor is rewarded with exaggerated laughter.

There were three presentations, two by company officials, and one by a very close friend. Slim was then given the customary gold watch, appropriately engraved on the back. He kissed Betty softly on the cheek, touched and squeezed her hand gently, and then moved to the microphone.

Slim was not known for his speech-making ability. He was a quiet, stocky, hard-working man. He stood silently, staring at the microphone. Then he lifted his eyes toward the gathered friends and neighbors and began. His words were softly spoken, but easily understood.

He gave a simple, sincere thanks to his family, his employers, his friends. Then he told us a story he had read somewhere a few months before.

"When Victoria was queen of the powerful British Empire, she visited the Punjab in India. Her empire stretched around the globe. Britain ruled the seas. When Queen Victoria spoke, the world listened. That afternoon in the Punjab, she was told that a young prince of a minor province would like to make a presentation to the queen. She said, 'Show him in.'

"The young man, just a boy in his teens, knelt before the queen. Then he stood, reached into his pocket, and held out a small cloth bag. The queen's attendant opened the bag. A brilliant, polished diamond fell into his hand. The audience gasped a little, each one whispering to the other about the size of the stone.

"Queen Victoria thanked the young man and promised him that his gift would become a permanent part of the Crown Jewels in London.

"Years later, the young prince made a trip to England. He asked to see the aging Queen Victoria. She was reminded of the young man's gift and granted him an audience almost immediately. After proper introductions, the young man asked if he might see the diamond he had given to the queen. It was brought from the vault and handed to him. "Your Highness," he said, "Years ago when I was still a boy, I gave this diamond to you with all my heart. Now I am a man. Now I know how much this stone is really worth. May I give it to you again, with all my heart?' "

Slim paused and turned toward his Betty. "I am not a fancy stone. Nobody would give many dollars for this weathered body. Once I gave my life to you. After forty-six years, the Big Depression, world war, Korea, Vietnam, two wonderful kids, three beautiful grand-kids, and a lot of scrambled eggs and bologna sandwiches, I know how much this life means to me. To our God and to you, Betty, may I give myself again, with all my heart?"

I think she said yes. She was daubing at her eyes and scrambling to get hold of her man.

An Unfair Load to Carry

....

Matthew 9:32-38
"And seeing the multitudes, he felt compassion for them." (v. 36 RSV)

....

 "A fifteen-year-old kid shouldn't have to carry that kind of load. It just isn't right," the pastor said as we drove toward his church.

"Now help me a little. I'm not following this story very well," I responded.

"Well, this kid's father was the football coach at

our college. Our town is small, about eight thousand folks. But the college brings in about twenty-five hundred students every fall." The campus was pretty, but deserted as we drove past. The temperature was just below freezing with a light drizzle falling.

He went on with his story. "College football coaches make pretty good salaries. But this fellow must have thought he needed more. Somehow he had a connection with a fellow in our capital city. This fellow was taking men's suits from a large store in the city. The football coach was selling them to his athletes here on campus . . ."

"So, the coach attracted athletes with good clothes at bargain prices and pocketed the cash, right?"

"Right. The big store in the city discovered the problem at inventory time. Their investigation finally led to our football coach. The news hit our town like a bomb."

"One more question. How was the coach's son involved in all this?"

"He wasn't involved at all. No one in the coach's family knew what was happening. But they have paid the price. High school kids can be pretty cruel. The coach's picture was on television and in the paper. He was forced to resign his position at the college. The whole family has just withdrawn from the community. They slip in and out of town to buy groceries. Nothing more."

He turned into the church parking lot and stopped the car. "I'm telling you all this because this story may have a good ending. One of the ladies in this church teaches the fifteen-year-old at school. She has had several long talks with him about his family. She begged him not to withdraw; to hold up his head; to study hard; to be open and honest and genuine. He has been coming to church alone. He was there last night and the night before."

In a few moments the church service was under way. Old, familiar hymns, a moving prayer by the pastor, and then time for my sermon. I preached what I was prepared to preach, of love, forgiveness, a new look at life.

As we stood to sing the closing hymn, one lonely figure started down the aisle toward the altar. He looked so young, so thin and afraid, so alone. Faces turned toward him, continuing their song. And then a lady moved into the aisle alongside him, fell into step as he moved on toward the altar. Not his mother or sister or aunt—but his teacher from school. She stood beside him as he was baptized. She was first to greet him as a new member of Christ's church.

Then others came, and others after them. Some were fellow students, some older, some younger. Some shook his hand, some hugged him, but all felt for him and with him.

Matthew wrote, "Jesus went round all the towns and villages teaching in their synagogues, announcing the good news of the kingdom, and curing every kind of ailment and disease. The sight of the people moved him . . ."

Courage Is Not Always Loud

Psalm 22:1-24
"but when he cried to Him for help, He heard." (v. 24 RSV)

 "Robbing and stealing are not new," she said. "I can tell you a story older than I am to show you what I mean."

My ninety-year-old grandmother was telling us some of her favorite stories.

"I was born in 1885. That's a long time ago. But twenty years before that, my mama was a young girl. The War Between the States was grinding down, almost over," she went on. "As soldiers deserted or were released, they sometimes gathered into bands of renegades. Some of them robbed only for food. Others might take your cows, chickens, horses, or mules. A few even hurt women and little children."

We all sat close around her. I had heard this story many times before, but Gayle and the children had not.

"My grandfather and the older boys were away at war. My grandma, my mama, and the younger children lived in fear of those roving bands. Even if they did not hurt anyone in the house, losing your animals and food was terrible. There were no grocery stores and no money to buy more. One afternoon late my mama was gathering eggs from the hen house. She heard their old horse snort in the pasture. On the hill west of the farm, she saw six or eight men riding hard.

"She screamed for her mother and ran to the house. They had only a couple of minutes to round up the children and lock every door. They hid the smaller children in a back room. Then my mama and grandma went into the front room of the house. The sun was going down. The room was almost dark with the door shut and locked. They could hear their own breathing. Then the sound of horses, closer and closer. The horses stopped within a few feet of the front porch. Through a crack in the door facing, the two could see six men. They were dirty, bearded, and loud. One jumped down off his horse. He took off his hat, beat some of the dust off his clothes.

"There wasn't a gun in the house. Our men folk had taken the guns with them. Two ladies and no gun against six men who were heavily armed.

"The man on the ground called out, 'Open the door! We want food! Now!'

"My grandma reached in her apron pocket and took out her scissors. My mama told how foolish that seemed to her at the time. What could one woman do with one pair of scissors against six armed men? But those men couldn't be sure how many people or guns might be inside the house.

"My grandmother's hands were shaking in fear, but she steadied one against the other.

"The men outside were quiet, waiting for an answer. Carefully, my grandma clicked the blades of the scissors together, imitating the hammer action on a gun. At the same time she took a deep breath and hollered, 'We mean you no harm, but the first man who steps on that porch—I'll blow his head off.' They mumbled to each other, afraid to call her bluff. Their leader mounted his horse, and they rode off.

"Grandma gathered all her children together, putting her arms around the little circle. Then she prayed, thanking God for courage and asking him to bring our men home safe and soon.

"Later as she peeled potatoes for supper, my mama saw her cry just a little."

The Kid Bubbles

Psalm 84:1-12
"Even the sparrow finds a home, and the swallow a nest for herself" (v. 3 RSV)

The kid is only two, barely two, but he bubbles with personality, and rightly so. His mother is a former Miss University of Alabama. His father was twice chosen for Who's Who in American Colleges and Universities. One grandfather is a trial lawyer, a past president of the Alabama Bar Association. The other grandfather is one of Alabama's most successful real estate men.

Ben has dark brown eyes with long, curly eyelashes.

He is soft and round, and waddles when he walks. A handsome olive complexion fades upward into a soft, windblown tousle of hair. He draws a crowd.

I had met his mother and father only once before, briefly, at a Rotary International Convention in New Orleans. A few months later his father had asked me to come and preach a three-day series of sermons at his church. Ben had not attended the banquet I addressed in New Orleans, so I saw him for the first time at the airport more than a year later.

"Mouzon, we have time to get something to eat before church. What do you like?" his dad had asked.

"What does Ben like?" I had responded.

"Ben likes food. How about seafood?"

Before our food arrived at the table, Ben had decided to explore a little. He came back with a french fried potato dangling from one corner of his mouth. His mother scolded him a little, but a lady at the next booth said, "Who could resist those eyes?"

He disappeared again. His mother and father were telling me all about their church, their home, and the enthusiasm of their congregation for the preaching services about to begin.

A waitress appeared with our food. Another was holding Ben. He was holding a small glass, sipping a light pink liquid through a tiny little straw, the kind one usually associates with a lounge.

"What is he drinking?" his dad asked the waitress.

"Our bartender has a special for little kids—ginger ale and cranberry juice."

Ben was obviously enjoying himself. He tackled his fish with gusto.

43

I spoke five times in forty-eight hours. Those sermons were layered around two meals at the church, two meals in parishioners' homes, and three afterglows of punch and cookies. Visiting went on until midnight both nights. Ben's usual routine was shot. He could not get to sleep. He was afraid he would miss something important. He laughed, he ate, he jumped, he ran, his eyes sparkled.

Then just before the last service, Ben started to cry. He wanted his daddy to hold him, then his mom, then his dad, then his mom. His mother ate her evening meal with Ben stretched across her lap, feeding herself with one hand, thumping Ben's bottom with the other until his sobs died away and he fell asleep. He had no fever. He did not seem to be sick, but this was a definite change in behavior. His folks were noticeably concerned.

As Michael drove me to the airport early the next morning, I asked, "How is Ben this morning?"

"Ben's fine. He slept about ten hours and woke up in great shape."

He drove on in silence and then added, "I should have been more sensitive, more aware. Late yesterday I carried him to the church nursery, so Margaret could attend another meeting. Ben usually loves to go to the church. He knows all the other kids. All the ladies know him. But he did not want to go yesterday. He didn't cry, but when I started to help him out of the car, he pointed one chubby finger at his own tummy and said, " 'Me-home. Me-home.' He had just run his battery down and seemed to know it. He just wanted to go home."

I understand the feeling, though it means something slightly different every year.

When Now Seems to Be Forever

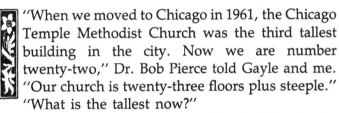

Psalm 103:1-13
"As the heavens are high above the earth, so great is his steadfast love." (v. 11 RSV)

"When we moved to Chicago in 1961, the Chicago Temple Methodist Church was the third tallest building in the city. Now we are number twenty-two," Dr. Bob Pierce told Gayle and me. "Our church is twenty-three floors plus steeple."

"What is the tallest now?"

"The Sears Tower—it is the tallest building in the world. Maybe tomorrow the clouds will break up and you can take a tour. On an overcast day, it is a waste of time to go to the top."

Snow fell part of that afternoon. The clouds hugged the ground all day. But Thursday was definitely better. By midmorning, the fog had burned away, and the sun peeped through.

The Sears Tower is huge, to say the least. I had to stand six blocks away to get the whole building in the viewfinder of my camera. We were accustomed to seeing the Houston skyline with its tallest building of fifty-four floors. The Sears Tower has 103. The observation level has wide, spacious walking areas, all glass-enclosed, permitting a full view from all four directions.

We could hear visitors from other states picking out points of interest: the old water tower, one of the few structures left standing after the Chicago Fire of 1871; the Prudential Building, Chicago's tallest for many years; the original site of the stockyards; Lake Michigan; the Loop, the fork in the river; Midway Airport; way out on the horizon, O'Hare Field, busiest airport in America; Museum of Natural Science; the Chicago Temple; the Picasso Sculpture at City Hall; the Calder Sculpture at the Federal Building; the Marc Chagall *Four Seasons* mural; Soldier Field; Wrigley Field; parks, the zoo, the Chicago elevated, Marshall Field's, bike trails on the icy shoreline, wandering condominiums along the lakefront. The sun sparkled in the cold air, promising spring to the long-dormant trees outlining the nearest houses.

That afternoon we flew home to the Gulf Coast. There, the warm winds of March had been chilled by soft night breezes. A heavy, wet fog covered everything, but we had one more long hour ahead, a foggy drive along Interstate 10.

"Hey, Eastbound," a trucker crackled into his radio, "How far does this stuff run?"

"You got a good two hundred miles just this bad, Astrodome city to Baton Rouge. How about your tailpipes?" another answered.

"No better that way, either. It has been awful bad. It

looks like a long night, rascal. Just hang in there."

The interstate had reflectors marking the lanes east and west. When my front bumper reached one reflector, my headlights could barely reach the next one hiding in the fog. I hoped the traffic engineers had not left a gap somewhere. "There is no chance that someone could miss a ramp and get into the westbound lanes while heading east, is there?" I thought. "Surely there is no one on this road without good, strong tail lights, no one stopped on the pavement to fix a flat, no cow or horse loose on the right of way." As my car slid through one small opening in the fog, a larger, denser patch reached out to swallow me up. Even the trees and fences, oncoming traffic, and fellow travelers were enveloped. It was like flying through clouds so dense one cannot see the ends of the wings, only rosy cotton candy where there must be light.

I pushed on, breathing, "Thank you, Father, for those moments when we stand in a higher place and feel that we can see forever. Thank you even more for being there when we cannot see nor feel a future, when now seems to be forever."

Which Had the Better Thanksgiving?

James 1:16-25
"Every perfect gift is from above." (v. 17 RSV)

"Dad, look!" Jason said suddenly, his finger pointing down the street toward our house. "Look at the paper. We have been wrapped." Soggy, wet toilet tissue covered our trees.

I turned into the driveway and got out of the car. Our mailbox had been beaten to the ground.

My heart sank. Thanksgiving Day had been the first opportunity to go visit our parents since July 4. We had left our yard looking so pretty. The Saturday before, the five of us had raked for more than three hours, filling thirty-three huge bags with leaves and pine straw. I hurried around to the back of the house where we had left those bags. Thirty-two of them had been ripped apart and scattered across the yard. Only one remained intact.

We had left the bags stacked against the back of the house on the sidewalk, waiting for the fourth Tuesday pickup of dry trash.

"What are we going to do?" Trey asked.

"Well, let's rake leaves now. We can unload the car later. But we will have to hurry. I have a wedding to perform in a little more than an hour."

"We used the last bag we had. Somebody will have to go and buy more bags," Gayle reminded me. "You go. The four of us will start raking and pulling paper off the trees."

We raked and sacked leaves, stripped paper from the trees, tried to repair the mail box well enough to hold the mail until we could do something better. When we had every leaf bagged, we had not filled even twenty bags.

"Hey, what happened to the rest of the leaves and straw?" I asked.

"Look in the garage," Gayle said.

I lifted the door and saw fifteen bags of leaves and straw, but they were not our original bags. They were definitely another brand and color.

"Who did that?" I asked.

"I have no idea. The Allreds, Bessells, Blackwells, and Tyrells were all out of town. They saw no one around the house when they returned, and none of them raked and rebagged our leaves."

I showered and went to do the wedding. When I returned, Gayle met me at the door. "I have one more surprise for you. Our vandal slashed all six tires and tubes on the kids' bikes."

Why? That mailbox was not hammered down by a small child. And yet, there was no robbery. The overall damage cost the Biggs family a couple more hours of work and about sixty dollars in replacement costs. Boredom? Frustration? In a neighborhood of fine schools, driveways filled with cars and boats, and a church on every other corner—why? "It could have been worse" was little help in understanding the twisted motivations, the idiocy of our unknown vandal.

Someone whose name I will probably never know defaced our yard and slashed all the tires on my children's bicycles. But someone else whose name I will probably never know stopped long enough to rake up and sack fifteen bags of the debris in our yard.

Which of those do you think had the better Thanksgiving?

"The Most Beautiful Place . . ."

II Corinthians 5:1-10
"Whether we are at home or away, we make it our aim to please him." (v. 9 RSV)

Carthage, Texas, has only five thousand people and few opportunities for "cultural development." I lived six miles outside Carthage the first eighteen years of my life. Special entertainment meant a trip to the Esquire Movie Theatre. As a result, I have been a movie buff as far back as I can remember. Needless to say, some movies have more to commend them than others.

Blume in Love is a movie that one would probably not take a nine-year-old to see. Its stars include George Segal and Kris Kristofferson. The opening scene shows George Segal as a successful young businessman. One day he has a very bad cold and decides to go home in mid-afternoon and go to bed. But he also decides to take his secretary with him. George's wife has a bad cold also, decides to go home in mid-afternoon, and finds George and the secretary. She seeks and obtains a divorce. After the divorce is granted, George decides that he really did love his wife, that he wants her back very much. There is a problem; the former wife has found a new friend, a hippie-type played by Kristofferson. A large portion of the movie shows Segal's efforts to regain the confidence and love of his ex-wife.

Ex-wife, George, and new boyfriend are all struggling for meaning, truth, beauty. One night all three of them are looking out across the Los Angeles area of California. There are rolling hills, beautiful lights in the valley, fine homes, and fancy cars. Kristofferson says, "You know, the most beautiful place I ever lived was Brownsville, Texas."

That line brought a roar of laughter from the theatre audience. People in Nebraska may imagine a beautiful city on the banks of a fantastic blue river. But, that audience in Texas was very familiar with hot, humid Brownsville and its muddy Rio Grande.

However, it soon became apparent that the author of that line knew what he was doing. Kristofferson described a house, goats in the front yard, an elderly couple on the porch. The beauty did not come from the river or the goats in the front yard. The beauty had something to do with that couple on the porch. A "flower child" wandering aimlessly from town to town, remembered that moment as his most beautiful one ever. Could I name a place and time? How would my children answer? What about the members of my congregation?

Robert Schuller, a pastor in Orange County, California, reminded a group of preachers to "Bloom where you are!" Commit yourself to another so that she knows she can count on you.

Beauty is that place and time when one child of God struggles to touch and know another—grandfather, wife, friend, enemy—to be real, to love with no guarantee that you will be loved in return. No guarantee except from Him who promised that He loves you all the time.

"You Have to Describe Yourself"

John 1:1-13
"The true light that enlightens every man was coming into the world." (v. 9 RSV)

 "Will you answer ten questions about yourself and never use the same answer twice?" Jerry asked. "Sure," Ralph responded. Then he thought about what Jerry had asked. "Do you mean now, in front of all these people?"

"Right now. You just agree to answer ten questions about yourself and never use the same answer twice."

"Okay, I'll give it a try."

"Who are you?" Jerry began.

"I am Ralph Strump."

"Who are you?" he asked again.

"I am Ralph Strump."

"No, you promised to answer ten questions without repeating any answer. You have already given me that answer."

"Well, you had already given me that question."

"I did not promise that I would not repeat myself. I just asked that you not repeat any answer."

"Now I understand. Try me again."

"Who are you?"

"I am a husband."

"Who are you?"

"I am a father."

"Who are you?"

"I am a person who cares."

The questions continued, all ten the same. Ralph struggled to answer truthfully. "I am an American. I am a professor. I am a person who tries. I am a Christian. I am a taxpayer. I am a reader of biographies."

The two of them then discussed the meaning of Ralph's answers. Jerry and Ralph were trying to show a large group how important it is to know oneself, to know the priorities of your life. The next important thing is to decide how much of yourself you are willing to reveal to someone else. How else will they know who you really are inside?

Fynn's book *Mister God, This Is Anna* tells how a

small girl named Anna met a nomad one night. She was only seven. The old man was bearded, smoked a pipe.

Anna and her friend, Fynn, were sitting around a fire, listening to these night people talk. Anna liked Old Woody right away. She loved to hear him talk. She wondered why he had spent his life roaming the earth.

"Mister," said Anna, "Can I ask you a question?"

"Of course," Old Woody nodded.

"Why don't you live in a house?"

Old Woody looked at his pipe and rubbed his thumb on his beard. "I don't think there is a real answer to that question, not put like that. Can you ask it in another way?"

Anna thought for a moment, then said, "Mister, why do you like living in the dark?"

He gave a little chuckle. "My reason for preferring darkness is that in the dark you have to describe yourself. In the daylight other people describe you. Do you understand that?"

Anna smiled. Then Old Woody quoted one of Shakespeare's sonnets:

> In faith, I do not love thee with mine eyes,
> For they in thee a thousand errors note;
> But 'tis my heart that loves what they despise.

Leaving Before It's Over

John 11:1-10
"He stayed two days longer in the place where he was."
(v. 6 RSV)

The head wrangler was explaining cowboy cooking to the city dudes. "Those beans were old dried pintos. We boil some every day for several hours. Add a little chili powder, salt, tomato sauce, and garlic—anything you do is sure to improve their original taste."

The crowd laughed. They had just consumed several hundred pounds of barbecue, beans, baked potatoes, sour dough biscuits, and applesauce cake. They were sipping hot tin cups of very black coffee or cold cups of tart lemonade, waiting to be entertained.

The wrangler went on. "We used to boil that coffee in used sugar sacks. But then the sugar company decided to economize several years back by packing their sugar in cardboard boxes. So one of our cowboys hit on an idea. He went down to J. C. Penney's and bought a box of size 14 white cotton boot socks. They hold a good pound of coffee apiece. We tie up the top of the sock, throw it in a pot of boiling water. When the sock floats back to the top or falls apart, we know the coffee is ready."

His spiel included commentary on every item consumed, from the beef barbecue to the spiced peach. Then he paused and stared at the crowd. He spoke in short, deliberate syllables, "Now, we are about to pick and sing. Then we will have some authentic Indian dances before we pick and sing some more. We can empty this parking lot in ten minutes after the last song. Please, do not leave early. You have driven a thousand miles to get away from the city. Don't leave ten minutes early to hurry back to it."

Last fall we went to the local university's homecoming football game. There were princesses and alumni officers to be presented, beautiful band programs, and then more football.

The fellow in front of me was really enjoying the game. He had peanuts and binoculars, a red blazer and a pompom. With ten minutes left in the game, the home team had a crucial series of downs at midfield.

His wife said, "George, come on. Let's go home."

"Not now," he answered, "This could be the game."

"But I don't want to get caught in traffic," she whined.

He left.

Last weekend the five of us drove to the local shopping center for the July Fourth fireworks. This was our fourth consecutive year, and we knew it would be good. We found a parking place, walked several hundred yards to a good spot, and sat down. We had stopped at the super market for a bag of chocolates and fresh fruit, and we were ready for the thirty-minutes of bright lights and stomach-thumping booms. We were not disappointed.

Suddenly a family of four approached the car we were propped against. A little freckle-faced boy asked, "Dad, why do we have to leave now? The best is always at the very end." The man unlocked a door, the light inside disturbing the darkness.

"Get in the car. In ten minutes there will be cars everywhere."

The little kid climbed into the car, wiping his eyes.

In all of the Gospels, I do not recall a single time where Jesus got in a hurry, even to avoid a traffic jam.

Collecting Things—or Experiences?

....

Luke 12:13-21
"A man's life does not consist in the abundance of his possessions." (v. 15 RSV)

....

As the cable car slowed to cross Lombard Street, they jumped aboard. Gayle and I parted to let them slip into the seat. We were enjoying hanging off the side.

He spoke to her in German, "We made it."

"Yes," she said. "Climbing that hill was unbelievable."

"Sprechen Sie Englisch?" I asked.

Both smiled, and he answered, "Yes, I'm sorry. I should not have spoken in German. Do you speak German?"

"Only a little," I responded. "I studied German in college. Is this your first trip to San Francisco?"

"Yes," she said. "Do you live here?"

"No, we live in Texas."

"Texas," she said, nodding to her husband, "That is a place we have never been. Maybe we can go there on our next trip to the United States."

"Have you ever been to this country before?" Gayle asked.

"Oh, yes, three times before, but never to Texas. We have seen New York, Chicago, Las Vegas, Los Angeles, Miami, and now San Francisco. Have you been to Germany?"

"No, we have never been to Europe. Maybe we can go someday."

We introduced ourselves. He handed me a business card. It had the name of a radio station on it.

"Is this your station?" I asked him.

"Oh, no, I am just an announcer there. I have worked for them since college, about twenty five years. What do you do?"

"I am a Methodist minister."

He nodded and smiled. The cable car rumbled down the next hill and stopped at the intersection.

"Do you like San Francisco?" he asked Gayle.

"Well, I would like it a little warmer. When we left Texas, the temperature was ninety degrees. It is only fifty here, and this is June 9. But I love the beauty and the food. Are you enjoying the great restaurants here?"

He lowered his eyes and smiled sheepishly.

His wife nudged his ribs, "Show her what you bought for our dinner tonight."

He began to chuckle and unbuttoned his jacket. Inside, he had a package of German sausage and some swiss cheese. In a shopping bag, he carried a large loaf of dark bread.

"French cooking is so fancy," he said. "I prefer good sausage, cheese, bread, and wine."

"Do you travel a lot?" Gayle asked.

"Yes, we have been on five continents. Our most beautiful spot was Bali. But San Francisco is certainly a treat. You must come to see us in Germany soon."

"Well, so far we have seen only one continent, but we will save our pennies a little faster."

"Well, Reverend," he said to me, "we do not have a lot of money. Monica and I live very modestly in a small flat near the radio station in the heart of the city. But we decided our basic philosophy before our children were born. We decided that we would not invest our lives in collecting things that get older everyday. We are collecting beautiful experiences."

She smiled at him and squeezed his hand. At the next intersection, he said, *"Auf wiedersehen."* We waved back. "Be sure to call us when you get to Germany."

Today Is Not for Flying

I John 1:1-9
"In him is no darkness at all." (v. 5 RSV)

I was afraid the sudden thunderstorm would halt or slow down air traffic, and this was no time for a delay, not even a small one. I parked my car as close to the terminal as possible and ran through the rain. It was really coming down at the airport, though I could see sunshine just south and east of the main runway.

I had spoken at an early breakfast group in Dallas and was trying to catch a plane home.

"Miss," I asked at the ticket counter, "could you verify my flight to Houston and on to Beaumont?"

"Your name, sir?"

"Biggs, Mouzon," I responded.

She pressed the keyboard of her computer hookup, frowned at the answer she received and tried again. Her monitor lit up the way she wanted it to, and she smiled. "Everything checks out fine, sir. We will board in twenty minutes at gate 14."

"Your plane is on time?"

She pressed the keys again, waited for the answer, and then reported, "The aircraft is already stationed at gate 14. There should be no delay."

"Well, my connecting time in Houston is very short, and I must be on time today."

"There should be no problem unless the weather gets worse. Even then, takeoffs are no problem. Why are you in such a hurry to leave our beautiful city and run off to Beaumont so early on a Monday morning?"

"I am trying to get to Beaumont for a funeral."

"I am truly sorry, sir. A member of your family?"

"No, not really."

"A very close friend, huh?"

"Yes, a close friend."

There was no one else in line so early on a Monday morning, so I asked "You will keep me notified of any delay, should it occur?"

"Yes, I certainly well," she answered. At that moment, she noticed the gold cross set in the stone of my seminary ring. "Hey, you're a preacher, aren't you?"

"Yes, I am."

"This close friend must be a church member, right?"

"That's right."

"So you're not just going to a funeral. You are the funeral." Her voice got softer, "I just hate funerals. They are always so sad. Don't you think so?"

I nodded, remembering a young widow and three small children who would be on the front row at the church.

"I had rather sell airplane tickets. I make people happy," she said quietly.

"But my folks don't feel like flying today. They need somebody to hold their hands."

She nodded, "Looks like the storm is breaking, Reverend. I see the sun coming through that window."

A Museum All Around

Matthew 7:7-14
"And those who find it are few." (v. 14 RSV)

We wanted to see the museum, but food was first on the agenda. After a morning of tennis and swimming, food had moved to the top of the list. "Try the cafeteria at the Whaler's Museum. It is quaint and interesting." It sounded good, but Gayle and I figured the bus driver was probably a brother-in-law of the owner. Cafeterias of Polynesian food were not as inviting as they had been six days before.

"If you have had your fill of sweet and sour pork, try the sandwich shop." The tennis pro's suggestion won. We decided to find Ricco's Sandwich Shop. "Go one block north along the beach," he had said. "You get good sandwiches or pizza and the Whaler's Museum."

Gayle was also remembering the tour bus driver's final sentence, "If museums are not your thing, there are also thirty-six specialty shops for gifts and browsing."

The Whaler's Museum Center was easy to find, but locating specific shops was a little tougher. There was no central mall or directory floor plan.

"Pardon me, sir, could you direct us to Ricco's

Sandwich Shop?" I asked a little round man with an orange hibiscus shirt.

"Downstairs, south sidewalk, just past the macadamia nut ice cream store."

Ricco's was right where he said it would be. Gayle had Italian sausage and mozzarella. I had corned beef and swiss.

"Now, let's see the museum," I suggested.

"Fine, you lead the way," she answered. But then she spotted an interesting shop. While she looked for a gift for her mother, I looked for the museum.

I found a hat shop, a jewelry store, a candy store, and the macadamia nut ice cream store, but no museum. I asked one lady with a triple-deck cone, "Could you tell me where the museum is?"

"Museum? What museum?"

"The Whaler's Museum."

"Don't ask me. Maybe in Lohaina."

I asked three other folks.

"I dunno."

"Sorry, haven't seen it."

"Museum? Maybe on the upper level."

Gayle helped me look. We covered every sidewalk, looked at every marquee. Finally I spotted a small information booth.

"Could you direct us to the museum, please?"

"Well, sir, our museum is a little different. It is not stored in one building. Look over your head. There is a fossil of an extinct reptile. Look at the display case outside Ricco's, the mosaic beside the macadamia nut ice cream shop, the mobile outside the Polynesian buffet. Our museum is not a place. It is all around you."

Her voice trailed off a little, but just to be sure that I understood, she added, "Sort of like life, you know."

Remember . . . but Don't Live There

Acts 26:12-23
"To this day I have had the help that comes from God."
(v. 22 RSV)

"We have to hurry, or you will have to walk the last mile," our driver said.

"I beg your pardon," I responded.

"You ever been to Ocean Grove, New Jersey?" he asked.

"No, sir. This is our first trip."

"Well, the whole thing belongs to the Methodists. It is one square mile on the Atlantic Ocean. The Methodists staked it out in 1869. The traditions of the founders are still practiced. One of those traditions is that Sunday ought to be special. From Saturday midnight until Sunday midnight, no motor vehicles of any kind are allowed inside. It is just forty more minutes until midnight. After that, we will have to walk."

"Do lots of people come to Ocean Grove?"

"Oh, yes. Their auditorium seats more than seven thousand people. They have preaching on Sundays. On the other days they have concerts, ballets, musicals—they had Victor Borge a couple of weeks ago. Are you here on a vacation?"

"No I am here to preach four times."

"Well, they have invited lots of preachers here through the years. Old timers remember when Billy Sunday preached in that auditorium. Where are you from?"

"Texas," I answered. He did not respond.

He drove along Ocean Avenue and stopped in front of the hotel. It was old, but freshly painted.

"Old hotels here," he began again. "I guess everything in Texas is new, not in New Jersey. Ocean Grove holds onto old things."

We stopped on the sidewalk. He said, "You see those hotels? Everyone of them was built in the nineteenth century. See that scroll work on the fronts of the houses? Victorian architecture."

I noticed the long rows of benches along the boardwalk, the rows of rocking chairs on the hotel porch facing the Atlantic. Most of the guests were older, retired folk. Most of the rooms were already dark.

Our three days in Ocean Grove were fun. Sunday was quiet. There were no cars or motorcycles of any kind. No swimming was allowed on Sunday. But people came to church, and they enjoyed walking along the boardwalk or visiting in their rocking chairs. Our room had no television and no air conditioning. Our bathtub was the old kind, perched high on four legs.

Monday was a beautiful sunny day. The beaches filled with people. Early Tuesday morning, from daylight to noon, was "boy's day" on the fishing pier. My Trey wanted to be a part, so I watched him and thirty-five other youngsters casting away at the surf. The members of the fishing club sponsored boy's day every week. The club provided free bait, hooks, sinkers, and advice.

One old gentleman had brought his rocking chair to the pier. He sat down next to me.

"You see that kid in the blue shirt?" he asked. "He's fishing right where I caught the big one. It weighed forty-eight pounds."

"Wow," I said "when did you catch him?"

"In July—July 10—in '46," he answered.

That made me sad. Were all these folks living in 1946?

But another fellow leaned toward me and whispered, "Do you know how old he is? He was ninety last month. And he comes down here at daylight every Tuesday to try to teach somebody else's kid how to catch a fish."

That night the tabernacle was filled to capacity. Some stood around the walls.

I saw my new friend from the pier, his mouth wide open as we all sang,

I love to tell the story, for those who know it best,
seem hungering and thirsting to hear it like the rest.

"I Get Lonely Out Here"

John 16:24-33
*"Yet I am not alone, for the Father is with me." (v. 32
RSV)*

"Lucky Dollar, where are you, rascal?"

"I'm coming to a lollypop right now. I know I'm almost to the Winnie-town—822. Bring yourself on up here."

"I'm hurrying, but my rig won't go that fast. I'm just trying to stay close to you."

"Roger," the trucker answered. "At least all the four-wheeled good-buddies have gone home to bed. The road belongs to us eighteen-wheelers."

I was driving along Interstate 10, listening to the radio to pass the long miles.

The first one keyed his mike again and said, "Lucky Dollar, it has been a long week, and I am ready to get home to momma."

"What if momma's not at home when you get there?"

"Oh, she'll be home. She got off at eleven. She works the evening shift, so she has had plenty of time to get home. Where's your home, twenty?"

"Alabama," Lucky Dollar responded, "a little town near Birmingham."

"How long have you been gone from momma?"

"I've been gone from Alabama about five days. The

boss sent me to Dallas, then Brownsville, then Houston. Now I'm on the way to Super Dome City, then on to Alabama.

"Well, momma will be looking good to you by the time you get back."

"Roger, only problem is that I don't live with momma anymore. We finally gave up on each other three years ago."

"Sorry, I didn't mean to be so nosy."

"No harm done," he answered. There was a long pause; then he asked, "You got any kids?"

"No, not yet. You?"

"Yeah, two boys. They live with their mother in Alabama. I send them $200 a week. I told their mother she better not start working while our boys were still in school. If she ever did, I would file charges against her for being an unfit mother. Then I would take the boys and move out to a little eighty-acre farm I have in northern Alabama. I couldn't make as much money farming as I do rolling this truck, but I don't aim for my boys to come home from school to an empty house."

"Do your boys know how many hours you push that rig over these super slabs to get that $200 a week for them?"

Lucky Dollar did not answer right away.

The Silver Streaker then asked, "Reckon their mother ever tells those boys how much you care?"

There was still no answer.

"Maybe you better go by and tell them yourself how much you care. You reckon?"

"I reckon," he said finally. "Say, would you pedal

that thing a little faster. When I can't see your headlights, I get lonely out here."

But Henry Is Real

Matthew 6:5-15
*"Go into your room and shut the door and pray to your
Father." (v. 6 RSV)*

"Henry is hungry," he said.
I squatted down so I could look straight into two of
the bluest eyes I have ever seen.
Before I could respond, he said again, "Henry is
hungry."
He was carrying Henry by the neck, his right arm
squeezing Henry up tight against his own body.
Henry is a beige, fuzzy, stuffed dog. He belongs to
Brett. Brett is only two, my youngest nephew.
"What does Henry like to eat?"
"Henry likes ice cream."
"Does Henry like barbecued chicken before ice
cream?"
His eyes danced, his head bobbing up and down.
"Good," I said. "We will have chicken ready for
Henry and Brett in two more minutes. Let your

mommy help wash your hands, and the chickens will be ready."

He waddled toward the back door, dragging Henry behind him.

Last night he had slept with Henry, his right arm squeezing him tight around the neck just as now. Brett and Henry slept on a bed made down on the floor in my boys' room. The whole Biggs clan had huddled close by the beds to say evening prayers. Henry did not pray, not out loud anyway, but Brett did. He called the roll of the whole family and thanked God for each one.

I remembered when our Allison was born. Our pediatrician recommended that we buy her a soft doll or stuffed animal with a music box inside.

"Every time you put her to bed, just wind up the music box and put the toy in one corner of the bed. Allison will learn to associate toy, music, home. When you take her to church or to grandmother's house, carry the toy along with you. If she seems a little apprehensive, wind up the music box and let her hold her toy. She will feel safe and secure, like her own home and her own bed."

"Allison named her dog Susie and wagged him everywhere. Susie was as important as blankets and diapers and baby food. Wherever Allison went, Susie went.

I looked at Brett and Henry lying so close together in their yellow sleeping bag. Henry's eyes were wide open, but Brett's were beginning to droop. As everybody filed out of the bedroom door, I flipped off the light. Right now, he puts a lot of love and confidence in old Henry. Henry is real and soft and dependable.

God is only a sound to him now. He prays because his mom and dad have taught him to pray and because he gets to call the names of some very special people, "Grandmother, grandaddy, Brian, Allison, Trey, Jason, Manuel, Miguel . . ."

I crawled into my own bed a little later that evening. I prayed that by the time Brett learns that Henry is only a stuffed, fuzzy toy, he will know that the one to whom he prayed is the One who is forever real and dependable and close.

A Great Idea—but, When?

Luke 6:39-49
"But he who hears and does not do them is like a man who built a house on the ground without a foundation." (v. 49 RSV)

 The discussion was purely academic. The President had not offered a job in his cabinet to anyone in the barbershop, but they were playing the game anyway.

"Hey, Zeke, what would you do if the President offered you a job?" one fellow asked.

"Well, I would have to think it over, of course, but I believe I would turn it down. Ever since Watergate, those Washington journalists think they are supposed to save the world from corruption. Now, if I had inherited a lot of money like Thomas Jefferson or the Kennedys, I am sure I could stand any examination. But I started with nothing. Anyone who starts with nothing and builds something big has had to shift a little money around. I mean, it is nothing that would send a man to prison, but you do not have time to cross every *t*—you know what I mean, like Bert Lance."

"Yeah, I hear you," the first man responded. "You have nothing to hide, but you do not want anybody to look too closely. How about you, Roy?"

"Well, Zeke mentioned Bert Lance, so let me start there. Old Bert got into trouble because he has new money. Folks with old money can afford to give up four years or eight years to work in the government. But folks with new money have to keep stirring it. The senate committee would not have reopened the Lance hearings if he had not asked for an extension on the sale of his bank stock. When he asked for another six-month extension, the committee and the press started digging for more answers. No, sir, I couldn't go to Washington. I just don't have my business in shape to leave it for four years. And I could not afford to sell out. My biggest appreciation is still ahead of me. I would just have to tell the President to call somebody else."

The first man nodded his understanding and turned to a fourth man, "Well, Jim, so far the President has two refusals. How about you? Would you go to serve your country?"

Jim smiled and said, "My answer would probably be the same, but not for the same reasons. I did not inherit any old money, and I have not made a lot of new money. My business would probably run fine without me, maybe even better. But I would not want to miss four years or eight years of my family. Ever since John Kennedy and Lyndon Johnson, members of the President's staff have been expected to give eighteen hours a day to the government, seven days a week. That is too much for me. Now, take my son, Dave. He is thirteen. If I gave eight years to the government, Dave would be twenty-one. I would miss all of his years as a teen-ager. Suzanne is eleven. I want to see her grow and mature. She is so pretty now, like her mother, and I do not intend to miss my chance to see her grow. Now you take Henry Kissinger or Jody Powell or Pierre Salinger—do you think they ever saw a Little League ballgame or took a kid crabbing at the bay? They never got a day off, not even Sunday for sitting beside their families in church."

"Hey, Jim," the first one said, "how long has it really been since you took time for a ballgame or a fishing trip or sat with all your family in church?"

His face flushed a little, he reached for his coat, and said, "Well I'm going to—this week, maybe."

A Reason for Being Late

Jeremiah 8:18-22
"Is there no balm in Gilead?
Is there no physician there?" (v. 22 RSV)

He knew he was late, and he was hurrying. The choir had been warming up almost thirty minutes before he came puffing into the choir room. A trickle of perspiration glistened on his right temple.

"Hello, Bill," the minister of music greeted him, "turn to page three. Put a breathing mark after the fourth word on line two. On page four, line one, put a hold mark on the second word—no breath there. Okay?"

"Okay. Sorry I am late. It's been a long day."

He was a huge man. His hair was a sandy red, sprinkled with gray. His face was full and round. He towered over the rest of the choir. He must have weighed over 250 pounds, all of it distributed pretty solidly from his wide shoulders down. His hands were large and calloused, but they cradled the music sheets gently as the choir worked on the last page of the anthem.

I was a stranger to this group. For more than two years I had been scheduled to preach three nights in one of Louisiana's strongest churches. The time had come. The church was filled. The ministers led the choir through the double doors into the sanctuary.

Later, when the benediction had been pronounced, the senior minister directed me to a place in the narthex where I could greet the members of his church.

After shaking several hundred hands, I saw Bill standing next in line. He pumped my hand enthusiastically and said, "Dr. Biggs, I want you to meet my wife. She is right over there by the door."

I turned and saw a pretty lady in a wheelchair. Her face showed some signs of slight paralysis. Her right arm and hand lay limp across her lap. She smiled and tried to talk with me. Her eyes sparkled.

After everyone else had gone, the minister of music said, "Well, I saw you talking with Bill and his wife. He works so hard, rushes home to bathe, prepares their dinner, helps her dress, and carries her, wheelchair and all, up the steps into the church. That is why he is always running late, but nobody minds. Betty had a severe stroke three years ago. Bill and she are convinced that she is getting stronger. We all pray that she is."

The second night I was sitting quietly in my place, thinking about the sermon I was about to deliver. A clear tenor voice filled the sanctuary. I lifted my eyes toward the choir loft. I could hardly believe that tenor solo was coming out of that huge body.

I was even more impressed with the song he had chosen to sing,

> Sometimes I feel discouraged
> And think my work's in vain,

But then the Holy Spirit,
Revives my soul again.

There is a balm in Gilead,
To make the wounded whole.
There is a balm in Gilead,
To heal the sinsick soul.

I glanced down the center aisle. A pretty lady in a wheelchair was looking right at his eyes. A smile crossed her face. She was so proud of her man.

A Big Man Far Away

I Corinthians 15:51-58
"In the Lord your labor is not in vain." (v. 58 RSV)

Detective Michael Cataneo
62nd Precinct
1925 Bath Avenue
Brooklyn, New York 11214

The envelope was plain white, inexpensive, and unengraved. It fit in well with the rest of my Monday morning mail. However, the return address caught my attention right away.

Michael Cataneo is not a personal friend, but I remembered the name right away. I first saw it in newspaper accounts of the arrest of the Son-of-Sam murderer in New York.

One of the wire services had picked up the story of Officer Cataneo. On the night of July 31, 1977, the one thing on every New York policeman's mind was trying to catch the killer. Even with all the press coverage and police work that had been invested in the case, no one knew the name of the gunman. Slowly, his attacks had grown in frequency. Every detail of every murder had been pumped into computers in an effort to build a profile of the person stalking the young women of New York. Every officer wanted to be a part of the solving of those heinous crimes. But Michael Cataneo and Jeff Logan, two officers of the 62nd precinct, were told to maintain routine patrol.

They were working deep nights, the graveyard shift. As they patrolled their beat, the radio crackled with information about major crimes taking place in the burroughs of New York. When would the killer strike again? Tonight? Next week? In the Bronx? In Queens?

Officers Cataneo and Logan could have spent their shift daydreaming about missed opportunities. Instead, they did the job assigned to them. Shortly after 2:00 in the morning, they stopped their car to ticket four vehicles illegally parked on a street. A few minutes later, the murderer struck only blocks away. Again, the getaway was clean, but good detective work the next week led to a car that had been parked illegally in the vicinity of the crime. The officer's name on the citation was Michael Cataneo. From that ticket, a suspect was arrested and charged. That ticket gave the missing piece that caused all the other clues to stick together.

A couple of weeks later, I told a television audience about Officer Cataneo's acceptance of a routine job, his diligence and dedication in doing the job assigned to him. His faithfulness to duty and to his fellow citizens had led to a much bigger contribution to his city. That broadcast took place almost two thousand miles from Brooklyn.

I tore open the envelope and read, "Through the generosity of Chief James R. Newsom, Port Arthur, Texas, Police Department, I received a tape of your television program on Channel 4 for August 23, 1977. My family and I were very impressed by your comments. We hope that your listeners got the message you were trying to give—the fact that I, as a police officer, or anyone else doing whatever his daily routine is, can make a major contribution."

He said he had played the tape for his whole family. More than anything else, I hoped his aged parents and littlest Cataneos had understood that in Texas their son and daddy was a very big man.

"What If Somebody Dies?"

John 14:1-14
"Set your troubled hearts at rest. Trust in God always;
trust also in me." (v. 1 NEB)

"Dr. Bass, what if somebody dies?" I asked.
"Oh, no one is going to die," he answered. He smiled, rolled up his window, and drove away. I walked slowly back into the office. It all seemed so fuzzy and unbelievable. Just three months before I had told my pastor that I believed I was being called to preach. Three weeks later I had graduated from high school. Then I had settled down to sell drilling mud through the summer months to make some money for beginning college in the fall.

It was a real surprise that Tuesday in August when I received a call from the Methodist District Superintendent.

"Mouzon, I have two little country churches almost halfway between Carthage, Texas, and Shreveport, Louisiana. The bishop has no one to send there. How about you?"

"But I have no sermons. I haven't been to college yet."

"I understand, but we need you now. You can go to college five days a week. Saturday you can visit your members in their homes. On Saturday nights you write a sermon for Sunday morning. You preach at the smaller church at 9:30 the next morning. Then you drive seventeen miles to the larger church to preach there at 11:00. In the afternoon you write another sermon to preach at 7:00 p.m. Then you drive back to college and begin a new week. We will relieve you as soon as we can, okay?"

I asked several other questions, but he had good answers, at least they seemed so at the time. I agreed to try. But I discovered two problems right away— people do die and superintendents forget to relieve you.

Nine days after our conversation, the phone at the little parsonage rang. The church treasurer said, "Mouzon, Emma Rozelle died a few minutes ago. Her family is gathering at the funeral home in Marshall."

I drove the twenty miles to Marshall. It was a hot, dry day in late August. Why wasn't I selling drilling mud in the Sabine River bottom? I had been to two funerals in my whole life. I had paid no attention to where the minister stood or what he said. Did he lead the casket or follow it?

I nervously adjusted my tie and walked into the funeral home.

"Bob," I said, "what are you doing here?"

"One of my members died. Hey, congratulations! I hear you are the new pastor of the Mt. Zion Circuit."

"Thanks, Bob," I said, pumping his hand, "could I talk to you, privately?"

"Sure," he answered. He led me into a coffee room off the main hallway. We sat down at a small table. "Coffee?" he asked.

I shook my head, "No, thanks. Bob, how do you do a funeral? Do I lead or follow the casket?"

"Easy now, one step at a time. First, you have to remember that death hurts. Even if the one who has died was a hundred and four, and everyone can name six reasons why she is better off, death still hurts the ones who have loved her. Second, remember that dying is a part of living. It comes to everyone, but God has told us that death is just one part of a bigger picture. That picture includes birth and growth and faith and love and death and eternal life. You will learn how to say all that better after a few years at the seminary, but for now you will have to use the best words you know. If you are sincere in your feelings for the family, they will hear. I'll ask the funeral director to discuss your other questions with you before the funeral."

I pumped his hand again, swallowed hard, took a deep breath, and went in to see the Rozelle family.

A Time for Standing Close

John 14:15-21
"I will not leave you bereft; I am coming back to you."
(v. 18 NEB)

I got through Mrs. Emma's funeral fairly well. After two restless nights and several tasteless meals, my first funeral had passed.

Saturday night I wrote a sermon for the two morning services the next day. Sunday afternoon I wrote another sermon for the evening service. That was unbelievably hard. With no college work or seminary experience to call on yet, I had told my two congregations everything I knew about the Christian faith in my first two sermons. Right at sundown, I closed my Bible, tucked my notes into an inside coat pocket, and started across the oil road to the church.

I saw a car parked at the cemetery gate. As my eyes moved across the graves, I saw one lone figure standing beside the newest grave. I opened the gate and walked quietly across the long afternoon shadows.

"Mr. Ben," I said softly.

He raised his head. I could see the setting sun reflected in the corners of his eyes. He had been sobbing quietly.

"Can I help you?" I went on.

He nodded. "Would you stand here with me a minute?" he answered.

I stood quietly beside him. His head drooped down again. He pulled a crumpled handkerchief out of his back pocket and daubed his eyes. Then he spoke softly, "Mouzon, would you say a prayer for me?"

He took hold of my arm and bowed his head. I prayed, "Father, you taught us how to live in families, but when we have loved so long and so deeply, death hurts so much. Help Mr. Ben and me to accept death as a part of a much bigger plan. You gave Mrs. Emma life, health, faith, and love, and now you have given her a place in your eternity. Help us to go now with peace. Amen."

He wiped his eyes again. We turned and walked toward the church, his arm still locked in mine. He was almost eighty. I was eighteen. We could hear the sounds of the evening prelude coming through the windows of the church.

I had to go to college all week and then call in the homes of church members on Saturday. When I went by to check on Mr. Ben, he was not at home, nor was he in church the next morning. Late Sunday I started across the road to the church. Mr. Ben's car was parked beside the cemetery gate. I could see him standing quietly beside the fresh-turned dirt and wilted flowers.

"Mr. Ben?" I called softly.

He waved and motioned for me to join him. When I got close, I could see his eyes glistening again. He rubbed them with his hands. Then he managed a weak smile and asked, "Do you have a prayer for me tonight?"

We locked arms, prayed together beside the grave, and walked across the dew-soaked grass to the church. One Sunday he prepared lunch for me. But every Sunday evening I met him in the cemetery before church time.

Mrs. Emma had died in August. The fall came and went, then winter, spring, summer, and a new fall. Mr. Ben went to sleep one night and did not wake the next morning.

I drove to Marshall to the funeral home. I was almost twenty, a sophomore now in college, a veteran of more than a hundred sermons.

"Mouzon, how great to see you again," Mr. Ben's son said to me at the door. "I will never forget what you have meant to my dad since mother's death last year."

I answered hesitantly, "If only this could have been seven years later after college and seminary. I know so little to do or say."

"Oh, Mouzon, my dad didn't need fancy words or elaborate explanations. He believed in God and God's actions on our behalf. Mostly, he just needed someone to stand close."

He shook my hand again, and we went inside to decide how best to thank God for Mr. Ben.

"Something No One Can Take Away"

Matthew 7:24-29
"He is like a man who had the sense to build his house on rock." (v. 24 NEB)

"My brother and I had big dreams. He would be a doctor. I would be a professor. Each of us had a favorite girlfriend we planned to marry. We would raise our families, save our money, invest it properly, retire at age fifty with our wives. We would build two beautiful houses on a lake and write poetry, our memoirs," he said.

We all sat at attention. Dr. Bruno Strauss was a master storyteller, a splendid professor of the German language and European history. He was tall and dignified with brilliant blue eyes. His hair was full, a little unruly, and completely white.

"Our plans were moving along right on schedule," he continued. "Then came World War I. Hurt, death, depression, then inflation. Our two families lived through the war, but we lost everything we had been able to accumulate."

He took a deep breath, his eyes looking back over the years, then went on, "We started again. It was no longer possible to reach our goals at age fifty. But at age sixty! Yes, that was it! At age sixty, we could be there. But 1933 brought Adolph Hitler and the Nazis. My brother and I were Jewish. I was no longer allowed to teach at the University of Berlin. My brother was constantly harassed by Nazi officials. We feared for the lives of our families. We had to leave all our possessions, finally reaching England and freedom."

He looked around the room to see if everyone was paying attention. Then he came to the end of the story. "My students, today my brother is still trying to heal the sick. I am teaching, well past my sixtieth birthday. But we talk, we sing, we recite poetry, we pray, and we know that life is good."

Dr. Strauss lived on one edge of the campus. Late in the evenings he sat on his front porch, his wife alongside in her wheelchair. They enjoyed the students who came by. He loved a request to recite a poem by Goethe or to sing an old fraternity song in German.

Remember Tevye in *Fiddler on the Roof*? His world was falling apart: daughters who wanted to pick their own husbands, a milk cart without a horse, persecution by the Russian government? On a bleak, rainy day, he and his wife loaded what they could on a two-wheeled cart and started down a muddy road. Behind them came the strains of a beautiful violin. Tevye looked back, saw the fiddler following down the road, and gave a wave of his arm. Old Tevye wanted us to know they could start over again and again. His prayer cloth was no mere decoration.

The bell rang. Dr. Strauss rose slowly at his desk. "My students, build your lives on something no one can take away."

"And That Road Leads . . ."

Matthew 7:7-14
"The gate that leads to life is small and the road is narrow." (v. 14 NEB)

The local funeral director would be my host. The pastor had written that "the funeral director has a beautiful family and a spacious new home. He has invited you to stay there for the three days you preach for us in Arcadia."

The pastor was recovering from surgery and had asked my host to show me around town, introducing me to the business folks. As we walked along the sidewalk, he stopped suddenly and pointed toward one of the older buildings, "That was my dad's funeral home. You see that red pickup in front? It's sitting right where the wrecker left their car."

"Whose car?" I asked.

"Why, Bonnie and Clyde's car. My father embalmed both of them. Right there in that building."

I thought of the movie starring Warren Beaty and Faye Dunnaway.

"You probably saw the movie. It didn't tell it right. Clyde wasn't handsome. He was little and puny looking. Bonnie was small, too, and young," he went on. "After the ambush, the law men didn't even take them out of the car. They just hooked a truck onto the front of it, pulled it to town, and stopped right there."

The next afternoon I went to the local sheriff's office and read clippings about that warm Friday morning in May, 1934. Then three local men, one of them old enough to remember 1934, drove me to the spot where a small monument stands. Erected by the Bienville Parish Police Jurors, it simply marks the spot where death came. Four law enforcement officers from Texas and two from Louisiana were hiding behind a dirt embankment along the gravel road a few miles from Arcadia. A local resident whose son had known Clyde told the officials that the two desperados were on their way to a hideout in those north Louisiana woods. A truck on top of the hill faked a flat tire. The car, stolen in Kansas a few days before, came to a stop. The sheriff hollered, Clyde moved, and the shooting began. Bonnie and Clyde never reached their weapons. More than a hundred bullets pierced the car. Photographs taken in the embalming room of the funeral home still show the horror of their death. Blood-stains, small bullet holes through their upper bodies—Clyde was twenty-seven, Bonnie was twenty-three.

As I stood on that hill, I felt a warm breeze stir the trees. I could almost hear that old car, chugging along the gravel road, the warning, the rounds of rifle and shotgun fire. One could almost smell the gun powder and fresh blood.

I remember standing on the hills of Vicksburg, almost hearing the cannons and cries of war. But I also stood in the chambers of the Virginia House of

Burgesses and dreamed of Jefferson and Washington. Men and women decide how they live. Sometimes they decide how they will die.

Not far down that gravel road stood a little white church, old but freshly painted. I could imagine a preacher, perspiration running down his temples as he talked about faith and love.

I thought about Bonnie and Clyde, and I was sad.

To Be Still Surer

Romans 8:14-25
"For all who are moved by the Spirit of God are sons of God." (v. 14 (NEB)

 "He died."

"In Kentucky?" I asked my caller.

"I'm not sure. I don't really even know the time of death, probably Sunday. I was calling to see if you knew anything about funeral arrangements or place of burial."

"No, I have no idea. Your call was a complete shock to me. I had heard nothing about his death. It must have been very sudden."

We talked a couple of minutes. Then I let the receiver slide back to its cradle. I slumped down on the edge of the bed. Dozens of memories flooded my mind. For fifteen years this man was pastor of the Grapeland Circuit Methodist churches. For eight years prior to that he had pastored the Deadwood Circuit churches near Carthage, Texas. He loved to preach in small country churches, refusing larger congregations offered to him by the bishop.

I was present when more than seven hundred churches chose him to represent them in the election of four new bishops. They figured he would know a bishop when he saw one. That was a big day for him, a vote of confidence and appreciation.

Two years ago, he asked our bishop to move him from Texas to the Appalachian poverty area of Kentucky. He felt God calling him to preach, farm, and do carpentry work there. Permission was granted. The last picture I saw of him was sitting on a roof, trying to help little children keep dry when winter rains came. He and his wife worked hard and planned well. Meager salaries were bolstered by farming vegetables, tending fruit trees, baling hay, feeding and milking cows. Each child worked hard to go to college.

I knew his son David best. We played football together in high school. David later played for Kilgore College and Lamar University en route to doctor's degrees in engineering and medicine.

But my fondest memory of Wilson Wieting goes back much farther. One week in early fall, 1952, he came to preach a revival at a country church near Carthage. I was eleven years old and had never seen or heard of Wilson Wieting. Revivals were mostly fun for me. Kids my age played tag every night before church, darting around the trees as dark came on.

I always went into church wiping perspiration off my face and poking in my shirttail. This visiting preacher impressed me. His hands were rough and calloused like the roughnecks who worked with my dad.

He wasn't eloquent or fancy or loud. He was quiet, almost whispering at times, but he said good things. He talked about sin, but he also talked about forgiveness. He talked about poor people rising above ignorance and poverty, about a God who helped make that possible. He talked about helping each other.

Wednesday night the two preachers ate supper at our house. He talked about his family, his wife, his children. He missed them very much, he said, even when he was gone only a few days.

That night I played tag with the boys, went into church wiping sweat and dust off my face, poking in my shirttail. But I listened hard. Even a kid could understand what he was saying about God. God is unhappy when his people are hurt. He wants to be close to his people and to heal their hurts.

During the closing hymn I walked down that aisle with trembling legs, but he met me near the front pew and hugged me. I knew I had done the right thing. I am even surer today.

Doing for the First Time

Psalm 121:1-8
"The Lord will guard your going and your coming." (v.
8 NEB)

Only four days before Christmas, he was facing amputation of his left leg.

Doctors had discovered a rare bone disease that would require amputation far above the left knee. He was only fifty-one, athletic, trim.

He smiled as I entered the hospital room. Earlier that morning I had been working on a New Year's sermon, trying to put down ideas about changes of life. You know, the change of years, persons, health, wealth, or politics.

I had decided my sermon would have three basic points. First, a simple statement that change can be fought just because it is change. Archie Bunker was a weekly reminder of this option. Every Sunday night he and Edith sang of great days gone by, no welfare, better cars, more responsible people, no pushy women, everyone keeping in his place, all issues clearly understood and easily determined—or so they chose to remember.

Second, there are folks who question nothing, stand for nothing, oppose nothing. Change sweeps them along in quiet resignation. They look into some other face, some newspaper, some magazine headline, begging, "Tell me who I am today." When in Rome, they do as the Romans do, no questions asked. Paul was severe with earlier Romans. "Be not conformed to this world, but be transformed by the renewing of your mind."

My third idea was to face the future with hope. The God of Abraham, Isaac, and Jacob is the beginning and the end of history. His Son said his way will win. As we have a part in anything lovely, honest, true, and good, we participate in things that never die, in things that win. He promised that his way and his people are not lost in change. They do not lose to death nor in death.

"How do you feel about yourself?" I asked my friend in the hospital bed.

"I am afraid, but not panic-stricken. I asked to have this surgery as soon as possible so I could begin the new semester in January with my students. I have never been a one-legged professor before, but my life has been filled with things to be done for the first time. I had never been a soldier until 1943. I had never been a husband until 1946. I had never been a father before 1948. Forty years ago I decided to give myself to God and his way. He did not remove hurt or pain or disappointment from my life, but he has preceded me into every new moment, waiting to multiply any act of faith or hope or love that I might perform.

"So, this New Year I will follow him as best I can, even on one leg. I'm eager to get on with it."

He smiled again and squeezed my hand as we prayed together. Enough said.

Exchanging for Something Better?

Isaiah 40:28-31
"The Lord, the everlasting God, creator of the wide world, grows neither weary nor faint." (v. 28 NEB)

The television newsman pushed his way through the crowded mall, interviewing the shoppers, "Was Santa Claus good to you this year?"

"Oh, yes, better than ever," giggled a woman in her late fifties.

"Then what are you doing in this mass of people the day after Christmas?"

"Exchanging. My daughter lives in Chicago. She hasn't seen my extra pounds since last year. I need a size larger, sad to say."

He nodded and moved on to the next person squeezing through the crowd, a man with a small calculator in his hand. "Sir," he began, "did you have a good Christmas?"

"You bet! Wonderful, just wonderful."

"Then why are you fighting these crowds the day after Christmas?"

"Well, you know, these little calculators are the rage this year. Somebody figured I needed one, I guess. Well, I don't need one. I plan to trade for a goosedown jacket."

Interview concluded, the camera moved on again,

"You, madam, did you have a good Christmas this year?"

"Yes, sir, very good Christmas. Well, we did have one sister sick in bed. My older son couldn't get a flight from the West Coast. Otherwise, everything was fine."

"Then why are you shopping the day after Christmas? You must be a little weary of crowds and clerks by this time."

"Well, my husband bought me a new dress, orange and brown plaid. It makes me look so wide, you know."

Another nod, another glance for someone to fill his last minute on the air, "Madam, would you visit with me just a moment on television?"

She blushed a little, showed a faint smile, and answered, "Please don't ask me a question about politics. I haven't had time to read a newspaper in two weeks."

"No, ma'am, I promise, no politics." She looked relieved. He continued, "I just want you to tell us why you came shopping the day after Christmas."

Her eyes sparkled, "Bargains! Don't you know about the sales after Christmas? I can get Christmas cards, wrapping paper, ribbons—half the price of what they were two days ago. I just love to hunt for bargains."

Christmas, New Year, new beginnings—same people, same hurts, same wants, same fusses, same game.

Why are we still shopping the day after Christmas? Are we really exchanging for something better? These tired faces, hopeful smiles, drained energies, deep hungers to be loved and appreciated.

The days after Christmas, Isaiah's promises still leap out to those who buy and sell and bargain and exchange, looking, hoping,

"Comfort, comfort my people . . .
"Speak tenderly to Jerusalem . . .
In the wilderness prepare the way of the Lord, make straight in the desert a highway for our God. Every valley shall be lifted up, and every mountain and hill be made low, the uneven ground shall become level, and the rough places a plain.
And the glory of the Lord shall be revealed . . .
He will feed his flock like a shepherd,
He will gather the lambs in his arms,
He will carry them in his bosom,
And gently lead those that are with young."
AMEN. (40:1-5, 11)

Why Not December?

....

Psalm 145:8-21
"In all his promises the Lord keeps faith." (v. 14 NEB)

....

 "Don't you people know Christmas is a pagan holiday?" the caller asked me.

"I beg your pardon," I responded, wanting him to go on with his point.

In an irritated tone he said, "Your Christmas comes from a pagan holiday. You ought to have the guts to tell your listeners that all this hoopla came from the pagans."

For six years I had been moderating a ninety-minute radio program every Sunday evening on Houston's KXYZ. It was called "Religion on the Line." The program manager chose the title of the program for two reasons. First, we sit in a studio taking calls from anyone, no place to hide. Pick up the phone, listen, respond. Some callers liked preachers. Some didn't like preachers. Second, we promised to talk straight about religion. Any question would get serious consideration and a straight answer.

For six years, every December brought calls from one particular group in the Houston area. Always the same, "Your Christmas came from the pagans!"

After several encounters with this group my guests had their answers committed to memory.

One very capable guest was Father Nicholas Triantafilou, Annunciation Greek Orthodox Cathedral. His answer, "As one reviews the indexes of the many volumes of the Nicene Fathers, he cannot find a listing of Christmas. In order to locate their comments concerning the Nativity, one must look under the words *Epiphany* or *Theophany*. *Theophany* means 'the appearance of God.' The more frequent term used by the church fathers is the 'manifestation of God.' The birth of Christ was celebrated on the sixth of January along with Epiphany, the revealing of God to the Gentiles, and to the astrologers from the East."

The western branch of Christianity was the target of our caller's barbs. In the Roman Empire, there were many sun worshipers. Sun worshipers grew very anxious in November and December as sunlight hours grow shorter and shorter. But near the end of December, they were able to measure slightly longer days. They had tremendous parties and celebrations to proclaim, "The sun is not dying or going away. The sun is coming back. Our crops will grow. Snows will melt. We will live."

The early Christians saw their faithful sitting glumly at home, hearing the noises of parties down the street. "Why don't we celebrate the true Sun? God who was here yesterday and last year is always willing to come new into people's lives."

The birth of Jesus at Bethlehem is a fact of history. The exact dating of that birth cannot be determined from early writings, but December 25 is a great time to remember that the one who put the sun in space is also the one who sent his Son, "that whosoever believeth in him should not perish, but have everlasting life."

Do What Helps You—and Others

John 3:16-21
"God loved the world so much that he gave his only Son." (v. 16 NEB)

"The thing I dislike the most is incompetent salespeople."

"No, the worst thing is those scroungy decorations down Main Street."

"I hate parties, parties, tired feet."

"My pet peeve is Christmas cards. I get so tired of sending Christmas cards."

"Cards, I can handle. Presents are what I resent. Business presents, school presents, church presents, neighbor presents, family presents. I'm sick of buying presents."

The talk-show host on radio had asked for callers to list their biggest gripes about Christmas. As I drove to make hospital calls, I listened to the complaints. Long lines, pushy crowds, charge cards, poor quality at high prices, inflation, recession, strikes, traffic, kids, noise, and weary bones.

Each time I had to stop for a red light, I jotted down a reaction of my own.

First, if it is true that lights and food and cards and gifts cannot bring the real Christmas, then it is equally true that those same things cannot keep the real Christmas away.

Second, if there is anything keeping you from the true spirit of Christmas, have the courage to get rid of it. If Christmas card lists make you ill, if remembering old friends with a beautiful card really takes more effort than you have to expend, do away with cards. Start clearing your calendar of anything that really pulls you away from Christmas's deepest meanings.

Third, add more of the things that help you. One of the ladies in my congregation has been very ill for three weeks. Her son lives two thousand miles away and cannot come home for the holidays. Her doctor has decided she will be well enough to go home eight days before Christmas. "The first thing I will do when I get home is bake a mince meat pie and a pumpkin pie with lots of cinnamon. Then our house will smell like Christmas." Add a daily devotion at breakfast, a quiet fifteen-minute prayer time just before the evening meal. Add whatever smells, tastes, looks, sounds, or feels like true Christmas.

Fourth, remember that Christmas means loving enough to give, as God loved so much that he gave. A young girl from my hometown grew up in the Methodist Home in Waco, Texas. Recently she said, "As I grew older I liked Christmas Eve best. As one of the older girls, I would get to stay up and wait for Santa. In those years he came to the home units in a big green truck, loaded with presents. That was an exciting time." Later she received a scholarship to study in France, "I went with a group to the midnight service at Notre Dame Cathedral. It was a great experience. After the service we had a wonderful breakfast together. It was the high point in Christmas for me."

"God so loved the world that he gave . . ." What does someone really need that you can give in his name?

You Can Handle Tomorrow

Isaiah 44:21-23
"Break into songs of triumph, you mountains." (v. 23 NEB)

"If you think third grade is tough, you wait until fifth grade. It's murder," she stated emphatically.

"Oh, yeah?" her brother answered. "If you can do fifth grade, I can do fifth grade."

Those lines sounded familiar. There was always some kid around to remind you, "You think Mrs. Ruder is hard. You wait for Mr. Crumpet."

High school football players scream at eighth-graders, "You think that was a hard tackle? Wait till spring training next year. I'm gonna break your head."

Every age has its group of folks who love to tell you how tough life is going to be next year. "You think little kids are problems? Big kids mean bigger problems. Wait till they hit those teen years."

Every parent of a two-year old cringes at the thought that the worst is yet to come.

I started preaching when I was eighteen years old. After college classes each week, I had to write two sermons for Sunday. I drove twenty miles to preach an early sermon to eighteen people. Many times I had to stop beside the road for a moment. I was so nauseated I knew I was about to die. But I didn't die. If preaching to eighteen people could make me that frightened and ill, what would a thousand do to me?

But Jesus said some great things about dealing with today. "Be not anxious about tomorrow. The day's troubles are sufficient for the day." He taught his followers to learn a little and grow a little every day.

Professors begin every semester with the same stern words, "Finals will be no problem if you keep up. Do today's work today. Study every day. Never fall behind. Build tomorrow on what you learned today."

The older saints of the church say that even that last river is not so tough to cross—if you know your guide.

You can parent a teen-ager well if you do a good job when he's two. You pass fifth grade if you work hard in third and fourth. You can tackle a senior high fullback when you're a senior if you could tackle an eighth-grader when you were fourteen.

James Michener's *Centennial* has a story about Levi Zendt and his new bride, Elly. Elly is an orphan. Levi is a family outcast from a staid, pious German settlement. The two of them leave their past behind and seek new beginnings in the unknown West.

They struggle to cross the Alleghenies. Their horses

labor to cross a four-thousand-foot peak, pulling a heavy wagon. How can they hope to cross the Continental Divide when they reach Colorado?

Michener answers that question, "The height of any mountain is significant only in relation to the tableland from which it rises. The low Alleghenies, rising steeply from sea level, were just as high as a ten-thousand foot mountain rising from a tableland of six thousand, eight hundred feet . . . if a man and his wagon could breast the Alleghenies, they also could conquer the Rockies."

"Even Al Has a Need!"

....

Genesis 1:26–2:4
"So God created man in his own image." (v. 27 NEB)

....

"Boy, I didn't mean to get in so deep," Henry said to me, shaking his head. "I never figured old Al would respond that way. I mean, I was just making conversation."

"What happened?" I asked.

"Well, you know Al. Never gets in a hurry. Never gets excited. Calm and cool, the unemotional type. You know what I mean, Reverend."

I nodded my head.

He took a deep breath and began again, "Everybody figures old Al just for business. He and Betty have been married nearly fifty years. Happy enough, I guess. But you figure old Al is not the romantic type. Dependable and honest and fair, but no lace and sweet words."

That's the Al I knew too. He usually wears coveralls and heavy boots. When he wears a tie, it looks two inches too wide and four inches too short, white shirt sleeves rolled to the elbows. Al and Betty's life had revolved around their one daughter. But she married years ago and moved a thousand miles away. Al never talks about her unless you ask. Then his eyes light up for just a moment. She comes home rarely. They have not been to her home in twenty-eight years. "Too far from East Texas."

"Get on with it, Henry. Tell me what happened with you and Al."

"Well, he was helping me doctor a sick calf. You know I ain't no good with animals myself. Al is good help, a good neighbor, but quiet and all business. He told me this calf was in bad shape. Probably wasn't going to make it," Henry mumbled.

Then he cranked up again, "Just to make conversation, I asked Al if he ever got close to any of his animals. You know, if he had a favorite pig or horse or cow. Al finished doctoring the calf and then answered my question."

Al had leaned against the fence, "Just once, and it nearly killed me. A big Brahma bull, white-gray, eighteen hundred pounds. He followed me around like a puppy. I could whistle from the barn, and he would come at a full run. I would scratch his belly, give him a few cubes to chew on. I could back the trailer into the lot and tell him to get in. He would walk right in, an eighteen-hundred pound puppy. Then he got sick. I knew he was getting on in years, but it was more than age. In all those years he had never looked so weak. I told him to get in the trailer. When I got him to the vet, the doctor told me to leave him there. He was going to die very soon. I stood there looking at him a long time, scratched his belly, gave him a few cubes."

Now Henry spoke for himself again, "Reverend, old Al began to rub his eyes, big tears wetting his knuckles. I didn't know what to do. I never expected that from old Al, I mean, he was crying. I felt awful."

The image of God, a hunger to love and be loved—a heart capable of deep feelings. Feelings rarely expressed, but always there, even in Al—even in Henry.

Potato, Potato

Galatians 5:22–6:2
"Help one another to carry these heavy loads."
(v. 2 NEB)

If youth is wasted on the young, wisdom is sometimes wasted on those who are older.

"Ma, tell Gayle some of those stories you used to tell me," I asked my grandmother shortly before her ninetieth birthday. I could remember sitting with her in the front porch swing on a hot summer afternoon when I was a barefooted kid. She loved to tell those old stories. I loved hearing them, over and over. Now I wanted my wife to hear them.

"Well, okay," she answered, "which one would you like to hear?"

"Any one of them. Your favorite, Ma."

"How about the story of the disappearing potatoes?"

"Yes, ma'm, that's a good one."

By this time eight or ten grandchildren and great-grandchildren had gathered around to listen.

"This is a true story. It happened when I was a girl, before the turn of the century. Times were hard. My papa was a farmer. Most everybody farmed in those days. We counted on our crops to feed us through the winter. We canned and preserved what we could. Of course, there were no freezers or refrigerators," she went on, glancing at the little ones to see if they could possibly understand.

Then she continued her story, "Potatoes were stored in a separate place, a potato house. We tied the onions along walls of the potato house. The potatoes, we put on the ground and covered with straw.

"One evening at supper, my mama told all of us children that some potatoes were missing. She wanted to know if any of us had been taking potatoes for any reason. We all shook our heads. We knew that those potatoes had to help us get through the winter. For several days, more potatoes disappeared.

"Papa decided there must be a thief in the community. He and my oldest brother would spend the night in the potato house. If anyone came to steal more potatoes, he would be caught.

"Early the next morning, an hour before daylight, papa heard the door latch move. He stuck a match to a pine knot, quickly and quietly. As the door slowly opened, papa jumped from behind the door. 'Who's there?' he called, thrusting the torch into the dark.

"The long white beard of our neighbor caught fire. As the old man screamed, papa threw his arms around him. Papa's own body put out the fire, and no one was hurt. As we came running out of the house in our nightgowns, our neighbor's face fell.

"He stammered for words, 'I'm sorry. I really am sorry. We tried hard this year, but our potatoes stayed too wet in the bottom lands. They were no good. I'm sorry. We were hungry!'

"Papa picked up the man's sack. He filled it with good, new potatoes. Then he put his arm around the man's shoulders and said, 'Come inside. As soon as these girls get their clothes on, we'll have some breakfast.'

Ma took a deep breath. When we all sat down to hot biscuits and ribbon cane syrup, I remembered something the preacher had read to us in church a few days before, "Brethren, if a man is overtaken in any trespass, you who are spiritual should restore him in a spirit of gentleness. Look to yourself, lest you too be tempted. Bear one another's burdens, and so fulfill the law of Christ" (RSV Galatians 6:1-2).

Do You Hear Me?

....

Matthew 13:10-17
"They look without seeing, and listen without hearing or understanding." (v. 13 NEB)

....

Hearing may not be understanding. Really hearing means more than recognizing certain sounds. One evening while Allison was still only seven years old, she came into the master bedroom, "Dad," she said in a low whisper.

"Yeah, Doll, and what can I do for you?" I responded. There was no answer while I kept removing my tie.

"Dad," came the same low sound.

"What?" I countered, slipping on my houseshoes.

"Dad," she said for a third time, waiting to see if she had my complete attention. I stopped and sat down on the edge of the bed.

"Okay, I'm through. Tell me what's on your mind."

"Dad, I don't think I'll ever grow up."

That's all she said, quietly, slowly.

My first thought was to say, "Why, sure you will. Eat your spinach! Drink your milk! Take your vitamins!" My second thought was, "Are you worried about dogs, cats, or people who die?" I'm glad I didn't blurt out either of those reactions. It seemed very important to let her say what was on her mind.

"You don't think you'll ever grow up?"

"No, never," she murmured.

I put my arms around her, wondering why she would begin a conversation that way. She must be trying to tell me that she wants to be bigger, older, right now. There must be something she wants to do, but feels trapped by size or age.

"If you were grown up right now, what would you do first?"

"Go to Astroworld," she said, eyes shining, volume zooming now. "Could we, dad? Could we go to Astroworld?"

Now we had something we could work on together. At the dinner table we talked to the others about a good day for a trip to Astroworld. How young we are when we learn to wear the masks, hiding our real feelings until we are sure someone is ready to hear and understand.

My dad used to say, "I want this yard mowed. Do you hear me?"

Communication is helping another person to experience what you are experiencing. At a new restaurant we order two different dishes and then say, "Here taste a bite of mine." Meaning, "I want you to taste what I'm tasting." "Look at that sunset!" Meaning, "I want you to see what I'm seeing." Or we whisper, "Listen. Hear that owl deep in the woods?" Meaning, "I want you to hear what I'm hearing."

Life is so much better when someone shares a bite of lobster thermador, the mist rising from a mill pond, a howl of a coyote on a nearby hill. Somebody has to say what's happening. Somebody else has to listen.

A dream, a nightmare, a win, a loss, a smile, a tear—a walk in the woods or down hospital corridor. Stand close and listen. Do you hear me?

"I Handle 'em!"

Deuteronomy 6:1-7
"And you shall teach them diligently to your children."
(v. 7 RSV)

The very young and the very old have a way of saying what's on their mind.

"Could I sit beside you, young man?" she asked as she slumped into the airplane seat on the aisle.

"Sure, have a seat," I answered.

"Sitting around airports sure makes you tired, particularly when you reach my age. I've been waiting here almost four hours."

I nodded that I understood and kept reading my magazine.

She obviously wanted to talk, "How old do you think I am? Be honest now."

I looked at her as if I were carefully computing an answer. "Fifty-nine. You must be fifty-nine."

"Aw, you're being nice. I'm eighty-two. Eighty-two this past summer." She glanced around the cabin. Then her eyes fell on me again, reading my magazine.

"Am I bothering you? Do you need to study or something?" she asked.

I remembered Edward Albee's *The Zoo Story*, a play about a fellow trying to read his Sunday afternoon newspaper on a park bench. A young man sat down beside him and tried conversation several times, realizing he was a bother, but hungry to talk. Finally he blurted out, "Don't you understand, Buddy? I'm going to be on your bench the rest of your life."

I decided this lady was on my bench to stay. I put down my magazine and asked, "Where are you going all dressed up on a Sunday afternoon?"

"Kingsville, Texas," she said, her eyes lighting up. She then gave me her opinions on Henry Kissinger, Betty Ford, airport restrooms, the energy crisis, and the Israeli weapons requests. "This younger generation," she went on, "they talk big about big problems, but they never get at the problems they could do something about."

I kept nodding my head. She had been talking for fifteen minutes, hardly taking a deep breath. She didn't want a conversation. She wanted a listener. I was hanging in there as well as I could.

"Let me tell you what I mean. The other day I was in the Galleria in Houston. There was a lady in there who had a small boy, about three years old I guess. He was tearing up the place. His mother kept looking at the merchandise, letting this kid run wild. I caught hold of his hand to save one pretty vase. He screamed and almost jerked me down. His mother looked around, smiled, and said, 'Don't look at me. I can't do a thing with him.' I fired back at her, 'Why not? You're four times his size!'"

She chuckled a little, pleased that she had thought of such a good put down. "If she can't handle a three-year-old boy, how has she got sense enough to pull a voting lever? Or cross a busy street? My kids never heard me make a statement like that. I asked

God to help me have healthy babies. After they were born, I never reneged on my job." She took a deep breath and settled back in her seat. As an afterthought, she asked, "You have kids?"

"Three," I answered. I saw a quizzical look in her twinkling eyes. "I handle 'em. I handle 'em," I said.

She smiled and picked up a magazine.

He Needed It Worse!

Mark 4:13-25
"The measure you give is the measure you will receive, with something more besides." (v. 24 NEB)

Barbecue and fried chicken and fresh apple pie—those sights and smells mingled on a warm fall day. Tall oaks and pines surrounded the beautiful little country church.

It was a time for remembering lots of things. The man sitting closest to me lit a cigar, leaned back from the table, and said, "You know, that bishop reminds me of my father. He doesn't really look like my father, but his manner, his gestures, his laugh. He makes me think of my father."

Bishop Paul Galloway had preached a splendid sermon at this site of Texas' oldest Protestant congregation. He was now eating and visiting with the crowd of people just ten feet from where we sat.

"That bishop is a good man. So was my father. My father was probably the best man I ever knew," my friend continued.

I nodded my head, wanting to hear the rest of this story.

"I'll just tell you one thing I remember that showed me the kind of man my father was," he said. "He was a rice farmer at Amelia, just west of Beaumont. That was long before the days of big tractors and airplanes in the fields. Growing rice was always a hard job. One cold, rainy morning when my father went to the fields, a slow penetrating mist fell all day."

A lady interrupted his story asking us if we would like coffee. "No, thanks."

He went on, "Late that afternoon, just before dark, my father came home. My mother was cooking supper, but she noticed his clothes. He looked wet, and cold. 'Jim,' she said, 'where's your coat?'

"My father had already started toward the bedroom to put on something dry. 'Jim, you answer me,' my mother said, 'you left here this morning with your coat on. What happened to it?'

"When my father didn't answer her, she went into the bedroom, drying her hands on her apron. Then she looked in his face, 'Oh, Jim, you gave your coat away, didn't you?'

"He nodded his head, 'A man came by the field late this afternoon. He was wet and cold. He didn't have a warm bed or a hot supper waiting for him. He had miles still to go. I gave him my coat.'

"My mother scolded him a little. Times were hard

for all of us. Coats were scarce. Nobody had any money. But I could tell by her eyes that she felt what I was feeling—my father was a good man."

Looking at my friend, I knew this story had happened sixty years before, but he had never forgotten. He could still see his mother and her apron, his father and the wet work clothes.

What have I done today for some child of my Father? Wet, cold, hungry, alone, confused, hurt, discouraged, lost—and miles from anyone who seems to care.

A Belated Gift

Psalm 119:101-112
"Thy word is a lamp to guide my feet
and a light on my path." (v. 105 NEB)

"Learn these verses by tomorrow and win a new Bible!" That's what she said. We were only ten years old, and her assignment was tough. The Twenty-third Psalm, the Beatitudes, the Lord's Prayer, and the Ten Commandments came to a hefty total. One day to learn so much—but a new Bible was quite a prize.

The next morning we gathered at the small frame church for Bible school. Our teacher asked, "How many can say the Twenty-third Psalm?" Three hands went up. "How many know the Lord's Prayer?" Seven hands went up. "Who can give all of the Ten Commandments?" Only my hand was still in the air. Her voice dropped a little, "Does anyone know the Beatitudes?"

"I do. I can say them all," I answered. Her eyes moved around the room. She saw no other hands. "Okay, let's hear them," she said.

I took a deep breath and began, "Blessed are the poor in spirit, for theirs is the kingdom of heaven."

From there I moved through the entire assignment without a mistake. She looked at me and then at the others. "Fine, now take out your supplies. We want to draw a picture of the Good Samaritan."

After recess and refreshments, all classes were dismissed for the day. I found my teacher and asked, "Where's my Bible?"

"Bible?" she answered, "What Bible?"

"The Bible you promised if I learned all those verses."

"Oh, that was just an idea to make everyone work hard. There is no Bible. Besides, I couldn't give you a Bible without giving one to the others," she said as she walked away to her car.

Hurt, and then angry, I felt a need to cry and a desire to strike back—but I was only ten. When I got home I told my parents, "She lied. She didn't have a Bible. How can she teach Bible and tell lies? I'm never going to that church again!"

My dad had some pretty strong words for me, "We don't call our teachers liars. She must have had a good reason for what she did."

The next morning my mom made me go again. I went, but I wasn't happy about it. Every morning for a whole week they made me go.

Sunday was church day. Then home for lunch—on my plate at the table there was a new black Bible. Inside I read my mother's writing, "This little gift is not a reward for learning your scripture work, but a gift to remind you that we would go far to keep you from being hurt or disappointed. This little book, though small, holds all the information you need to make you a happy and successful man. All our love, Mother and Dad."

I kept it beside my bed, and promised myself that I would read in it every night, read it and underline my favorite words!

Little League, Boy Scouts, sacking groceries, algebra, girls, football games, chemistry, dates, good times, frustrating times, fun times, lonely times—its words came true. And when I was eighteen, I carried it into a pulpit for the first time.

When Ol' Tom Comes Again

Matthew 1:18-25
"And he shall be called Emmanuel . . . 'God is with us.'" (V. 23 NEB)

When my father was sent to Germany with the Army during World War II, my mother, my sister, and I went to stay with my maternal grandparents. They lived only three miles outside Carthage, Texas, but that was too far for public utilities. They had no electricity, no gas, and no plumbing. Kerosene lamps, wood-burning stoves, and a water well with bucket and rope served them fairly well.

Christmas time was looking sad with my father so far away. I was young enough that I had no idea where Germany was, but I knew it wasn't where we were. He was not with us.

My grandpa hitched the mule to a slide. A slide resembles a sled except that it was homemade and could run on dirt instead of ice. He hauled lots of firewood for warm winter fires and then started walking to town. It was dark when he got home. I was too sleepy to be very interested in the packages he brought inside the house.

The next morning at breakfast Pa Hightower said, "Did anyone hear a strange noise last night? A couple of weeks before Christmas Ol' Tom usually visits us."

I had no idea who Ol' Tom was. We had no relatives

named Tom, at least none that I could remember.

My grandpa continued, "When Ol' Tom comes to see us, he usually leaves a few presents around to let us know that Christmas is close. Let's see if we can find any presents."

This was only four weeks before my fourth birthday, so I was very excited about looking for surprise gifts. Behind the kitchen door, we found a huge grapefruit. Near the fireplace in the living room, we found an orange. The next day there was an apple behind the bedroom door, and a few nuts near the water bucket on the back porch. My grandpa had as much fun as I finding goodies left by Ol' Tom!

When the war was over my dad came home, and we moved away. But the tradition moved with us. Every year, a couple of weeks before Christmas, Ol' Tom brought Christmas goodies to the Biggs house.

I never realized just how much this fun meant to us until Christmas of 1967. My brother was in the jungles of Vietnam, stationed with the Fourth Infantry at Pleiku. My family in Houston mailed a box of goodies, hoping they would arrive a couple of weeks before Christmas. My sister mailed a package from Clear Lake City, not knowing what we had done in Houston. My mother and father sent a third box from Carthage.

Each of us received a letter from my brother, "Today I received three boxes of goodies. None of the three had a name inside. I guess Ol' Tom must have sent them. That means Christmas is getting closer now."

Family tradition means so much when it reminds us that times change, years pass, but some things last.

Ol' Tom is for fun. God's love is for real. Christmas

reminds us that God loved us in Bethlehem. He loved us in 1944. He loved us in 1967. He comes in power in 1974 . . .

"Come, Lord Jesus, touch us again, we pray."

First, We Give Thanks

....

Psalm 89:1-8
"Thy true love is firm as the ancient earth,
thy faithfulness fixed as the heavens." (v. 2 NEB)

....

A new friend told me about an interesting afternoon he had recently. He had gone to a hardware store to buy materials for repairing a leaky faucet. He found what he wanted and walked toward the cash register. There were two people already in line at the checkout stand.

The man who stood first in line was very unhappy about the price of his purchase. He was using strong language to describe the President, the local congressman, retail merchants in general, and this particular business establishment as a prime example of inflation. The merchant apologized for the higher prices, and tried to explain how his payroll, utilities, interest fees, social security taxes, workmen's compensation, and item costs had all gone up dramatically in the last few months. The customer was not impressed. He threw his money on the counter, picked up his change, and stomped out of the store.

The second person in line was an elderly lady who had stood patiently, waiting for her turn at the register. The owner said, "Good afternoon, Mrs. Ida, how are you today?"

Before she could answer, he continued, "Please, Mrs. Ida, don't tell me how bad inflation is, I know already. Believe me, I know how bad it is."

She smiled warmly and replied, "You'll hear no fussing from me. I needed this tiny part for my refrigerator, and I found it here in your store. I remember a day when I had no refrigerator, no car to drive to town, and no money to buy a part for a refrigerator I didn't even have. Do you understand me? Today I have money and a car and a refrigerator. I'm very glad to be alive today." She picked up her change and walked spryly from the store.

Later that afternoon my friend drove home, still thinking about those two customers in the hardware store.

He kissed his wife on the cheek and asked, "Any mail for me today?"

"Not now", she said.

"What do you mean *not now?* There either *is* some mail or there is *not* any mail, right?"

"I mean you ought to wait until after supper. There are bills, and they are higher than last month," she said.

He thought about inflation, economic summit meetings at the White House, election day, Republicans, Democrats, price controls vs. no price controls, free enterprise, and bank accounts. Then he reached for the mail.

The first envelope he opened was a bill from the telephone company. His eyes moved to the bottom line, then up again to a listing of the long distance calls.

"It's bad, huh?" his wife asked. "What do you think we can do about it?"

Later he would be willing to talk about supply and demand, ways to cut back on government spending, ideas for better family budgeting. But for now, he said, "I am thinking how fortunate we are! We have a son who lives more than twelve hundred miles away. That is a hard two days by car, but we have a car. It is much quicker by plane, and we can buy tickets. Or we can pick up this tiny instrument and talk to him and Betty and little John as if they were in the next room. All things considered, this is a pretty special day God has given us. Right? Let's have dinner!"

Do Something for Somebody, Now

Matthew 25:31-46
"Anything you did for one of my brothers here, however humble, you did for me." (v. 40 NEB)

 "Help somebody have a better day than he's ever had before." The words were simple, and they were accurate. "Be doers. Do something concrete. Put pretty words into positive action. Don't just talk church. Be church." My sermon was taking shape for Sunday.

There was a knock on my office door. "Come in," I mumbled, not really wanting to be disturbed.

George, one of our custodians, said, "Mr. Bibbs, could I get my check?"

"Sure, come on in. By the way, would you give the others their checks?" I asked. I had each check in a separate envelope, sealed, with the name typed on the outside.

He nodded, took the stack of envelopes, and started to leave.

"George, sit down a minute. I need to talk with you."

Two of our custodians were past sixty years of age, and their working lifetimes were almost over. Two others were college students who worked at night. They had bright futures ahead. But George was thirty-four, had a wife and four children. His future was our church. He had no other. I was haunted by the fact that round steak and school supplies cost custodians as much as they cost preachers.

"George, do you think you could learn how to operate the mechanical equipment in the basement of the church? We have almost three hundred tons of heating and cooling equipment down there. It has to be turned on in proper sequence. Oil pressure, automatic pumps, manual pumps have to be checked often."

As I talked, his head sagged down. He let the words slip out slowly, "I don't know how to read."

"George, last pay day you asked for the checks. I gave them to you. You started down the hall. Rosie got off the elevator about that time and saw the envelopes in your hand. She reached for them. You pulled them away, shifted through the stack, and said "R". You handed her the right envelope. George, if you can read an R, you can learn to read an A, B, and C. Would you like to learn how to read?"

His eyes had brightened once but now fell away again, "I don't have any money."

"I can get some money for you. Would you like to learn how to read?" I asked again.

There was hope and fear in his voice, "Mr. Biggs, schools are for kids."

"No, George, schools are for people who want to learn."

The next Tuesday evening at 6:30, George reported for class.

The months must have dragged for him. But one Friday afternoon two years later, our preachers and secretaries joined all the housekeeping crew for a reception.

We were introducing the new foreman of housekeeping. When I called George's name, he stood tall and straight. His eyes were bright and happy.

The big question for me is not "How many sermons did you preach?" It is rather, "How many of my children did you help to have a better day than they had ever had before?"

Leave the Changing to God

John 7:53–8:11
"Nor do I condemn you. You may go; do not sin again."
(v. 11 NEB)

His name tag is different. Most doctors at Houston's Veterans Hospital have government name tags, "Dr. Smith, Urology," "Dr. Jones, Cardiology." But his badge is not like the others. It says, "Jorge Valles, Human Being." He is Spanish, tall, stooped a little after many years of struggling with alcoholics. He is a psychiatrist. His mustache is long and curled, a real handlebar, mostly gray now. He paces, nervous with energy, eager to see sick persons get well.

The announcement from Hermann Hospital had said "Seminar on Alcoholism. Resource Person, Dr. Jorge Valles." As a minister, I was familiar with his books and lectures. I wanted to hear him again.

After several hours of instruction for ministers, counselors, and medical personnel, Dr. Valles said, "Let's do some role-playing. One of you fellows be my pastor. I will be an alcoholic coming to you for help. My secretary will play the role of my wife."

Role-playing is a great way to learn, but no one wanted to be the volunteer. Finally, two ministers pushed a friend to his feet, and he walked forward to the stage of the auditorium.

"Fine, fine." Valles mumbled. "Be seated at your desk. My wife and I will knock at your office door."

When the minister opened the door, Valles began, "Now, look, Reverend, I don't have long. I'm here because my wife kept badgering me."

"Badgering you? Badgering you? Just because I say you have a drinking problem, I have to be the villain, right?" She countered.

"Well, after a long day, a man has a right to relax a little, doesn't he?"

"Yeah, you relax all right. You get so relaxed a Mack truck could come in the front door without waking you."

"A Mack truck sounds better than a nagging woman and a bunch of ungrateful kids," he yelled.

"Kids? Did I have kids without you? Do you ever help with them? Never!"

Several times during this tirade the minister had whispered, "Would you like to sit down?" When the couple kept screaming at each other, the minister struck the desk with his hand, "That's enough, Valles. I don't want to play any more."

"What's the matter?" Valles asked.

"How am I going to change anybody if he won't even sit down and listen?"

Valles's eyes narrowed, "Well, Mr. Holy Man, who ever told you that your job was changing folks? As I read that Book, it says accept folks and love folks. But changing folks is God's business."

"He Commands, and to Those Who Go He Reveals Himself"

....

Matthew 28:16-20
"Teach them to observe all that I have commanded you. And be assured, I am with you always, to the end of time." (v. 20 NEB)

....

"Funny how things stand out in our minds. I mean, years after something happens, it makes a bigger impression than another similar experience," he mused as we drove along.

His face took on a wistful look as he continued his line of thought, "One thing happened to me when I was eleven years old that I remember now as a real turning point in my life."

Our talks had always centered around present

concerns of his business or family matters. I really knew so little about his childhood. Suddenly he wanted to talk about his earlier years. I nodded my head to show that I was interested.

"An eleven-year-old kid doesn't need very much money, but I felt my allowance was completely inadequate. My dad and mom believed it was large enough, so I asked permission to get a job. Permission granted, I started looking for a job. The only job I could find was throwing an early morning paper route.

"I was fine. No problems in my first two weeks. Then one night I went to bed with the weather report on my mind. Probable snow, sleet, or freezing rain.

"The next morning my alarm went off. I pulled back a corner of the drapery. It was really coming down outside. I pulled the covers over my head."

"Bud, time to deliver papers," my mom said.

"Oh, Mom, I feel terrible. My stomach hurts." She left the room. I pulled the covers over my head again. Then I heard heavier footsteps; my dad was coming. He was firm, "Bud, you have a job now. Get up and deliver papers."

"I dressed, got my papers, and started down the street. After throwing half my route, I came to a corner. I sat down on the curb, rubbing my hands together. I thought about throwing the rest of my papers in the gutter across the street, hurrying home to my warm bed. But I knew it would be only a matter of time until someone called and complained to my dad. I got on with my job.

"As I came to the last house on my route I was suddenly aware of a car parked beside the curb, lights on, motor running. I remember thinking, 'What nut is out on a cold morning like this who doesn't have a paper route?'

"Then the window rolled down, and I heard my father's voice, 'Hey Bud, how about some hot chocolate with me?'

"As I slid into the front seat of the car, sleet falling on the roof, hot chocolate pouring from the thermos, I knew my father in a way I had never known him before."

After Dr. Albert Schweitzer's lengthy search for the historical Jesus, he contended that Jesus lived. He comes, as he did of old. He commands, and to those who go, he reveals himself in the ineffable mysteries of life as to who he really is.

He Looked So Hard for Joe

Luke 15:1-7
"Does he not leave the ninety-nine in the open pasture and go after the missing one?" (v. 4 NEB)

 Toss a biscuit, and old Joe could catch it before it hit the ground. Dad said Joe was the best birddog in East Texas.

He was white from nose to tail except for one brown spot on his head and ear. Most of the time old Joe romped around inside a pen. But on cool overcast days Dad put Joe on an exercise chain. He could play, rest, or jump around on the end of the light thirty-foot chain.

One afternoon in early spring, I got off the school bus and went round the house to see Joe. Dad had asked me to hook him to the chain early that morning and put him back in his pen for nighttime. Wrestling that birddog in and out of the pen was a pretty big job for a ten-year-old.

When I turned the corner of the house, Joe was not there. I ran to the chain. It was broken. Only ten feet of the chain was still anchored. The rest of it was gone. I ran to the oil company office building where my dad worked, only fifty yards from our house.

"Dad, Dad, Joe's gone. He's gone," I gasped.

"Where? Gone where?"

"I chained him to the pole this morning, but he's gone."

We hurried home. Dad examined the chain, "Joe is probably just running in the woods. He knows the way home. The only thing that worries me is the twenty feet of chain he's dragging."

We drove along the roads near our home, calling, blowing the horn. We walked down pipeline clearings and crossed cattle guards and fences. No response from Joe, not a trace.

For three afternoons and two mornings we looked and called and whistled.

The next morning at breakfast, Dad said, "Joe is caught somewhere. He has no food or water. If we do not find him today, it will be too late."

When the school bus stopped at the gas camp that afternoon, I ran home and around the house. Joe was in the pen, thin and weak, but alive.

My mom explained that my dad and ten other men had combed the woods. Joe had jumped a fence. His chain was caught.

That night sleep was so good. If my father would look that long for a bird dog, I figured he would do the same for me if I ever got lost. It reminded me of a Sunday school lesson I had heard a few weeks before.

Maybe We Are Like Sheep

John 21:15-19
"Jesus said, 'Feed my sheep.' " (v. 17 NEB)

Sheep are dumb, some of the dumbest animals around. Now that shouldn't really bother me, since I do not own a single one. But I keep remembering how Jesus reminded Simon Peter to "feed my sheep." I know he wasn't talking about the four-legged variety. He was talking about people, about me.

Not knowing anything about sheep, I decided to do some reading. In every book and article I read, I found three central facts about sheep. First, sheep are dumb. My first reaction was, "Then people are not like sheep.

People are certainly not dumb. We discovered the wheel, fire, and rockets to the moon. Even a newborn infant can learn to speak a foreign language in the first eighteen months of its life."

But then I remembered how King David thought his affair was different and how thousands of businessmen and secretaries each year think their affairs are different. Nathan reminded David that adultery and greed are not new or different.

Children of alcoholics are more likely to be alcoholics, children of divorced parents are more likely to divorce, children who are beaten are more likely to beat their children. We are hurt and then hurt somebody else. Sheep are dumb.

Second, sheep follow a leader. If the leader is wise, all is well. But if the leader runs into a blind canyon, those who follow keep on following until they pile on top of each other, smothering each other to death. Our leadership took us to Vietnam, and we followed. After fifty thousand American deaths, more than two hundred thousand American wounded, and more than three hundred billion dollars, some sheep decided they had been led into a blind canyon. Yet those who questioned were often branded as disloyal. In their hunger to keep up with the flock, sheep follow into strange and foreboding places. The leader may turn to marijuana, promiscuity, escapism, streaking, or throwing cream pies. Sheep have a need to follow. "Simon, give them a better leader."

Third, sheep respond to tender loving care. The *Wall Street Journal* of April 30, 1975, contained an article about a former Marine who now heads a private school. He emphasizes discipline, courage, and self-control. But he said, "The North Koreans once poured ice water on my naked body at twenty degrees below zero, and I toughed it out. But a group of boys can present me a trophy with my name inscribed on it, and I cry like a baby."

This human animal responds beautifully to praise, encouragement, and genuine affection. From infants to cigar-smoking executives, they respond to real acts of love and kindness.

Sheep are dumb and easily led, but sensitive to kindness. They are difficult, but need care and attention.

"Simon, are you really my friend? Feed my sheep."

A Night Out with the Guys

Matthew 18:1-5
"Whoever receives one such child in my name receives me." (v. 5 NEB)

Helping buy clothes for three small children is a job every dad ought to have, at least once. Recently Gayle and I took our three to buy clothes. My day had been long and tiring. Trying clothes on our three was not my favorite way to spend an evening. But Gayle said she needed my help. After supper we drove to the shopping center.

To save time, I suggested that she take Allison and I take Trey and Jason. As I started to the boys' department, leading them through the Easter crowds, I remembered a similar night several years before when Trey was barely three and I led him into the boys' department.

I quickly found a young salesgirl to help us.

"Do you know what you are looking for, sir?"

"Yes, play clothes. Blues with blues, greens with greens. You know, just play clothes."

She was doing a good job of matching colors when I felt Trey tugging on the bottom of my coat.

I squatted down to his eye level and said, "Now, come on, Trey, no interruptions. The store closes in an hour. We have to hurry."

He said nothing, just let his eyes fall in resignation. I started looking at the merchandise again.

Two more sharp tugs on my coat—he had regained his confidence. "Look, pal, we have to hurry now. We can talk later," I said.

He looked at me with sad brown eyes, so I said, "Okay, tell me your problem." I squatted down again eye-to-eye. He said, "My Daddy, could I have some pants with pockets?" I looked at the pants he was wearing—no pockets. I asked the salesgirl, "Do you make pants with pockets for a three-year-old?"

"Oh, sure, they are over here."

I picked out several colors and took him to a dressing room. Why had he never had pants with pockets? Clothes manufacturers must know how many things those chubby hands had to stuff into a pocket.

As I pulled the first pair up around his waist, I said, "Oh, no."

His eyes got bigger.

"Now you will have to have a belt," I said. He smiled with pure pleasure in his eyes.

"Do you have a belt to fit these pants?"

"Yes sir. Lots of belts."

As I girded his first leather belt around his first pair of pants with pockets, I looked into his face. He said nothing, but he threw his arms around my neck, gave one sharp squeeze, and then walked out into the store. He intended to wear his new clothes right down that mall and home again. I paid the lady and then took his hand in mine. With every step, he grew a little taller. He was looking for his mother to show her how big he was. I'm glad I didn't miss that night. It will be special to me always.

Now I have two boys, one fat little hand in each of mine. As we walk into the boys' department, I say a quick and silent prayer, "Thank you, God, for little children, and for those special minutes when we touch."

Too Long Sick

John 5:1-15
"Among them was a man who had been crippled for
thirty-eight years." (v. 5 NEB)

 The longer you are sick, the more difficult it is for you to get well. Dr. Maxwell Maltz learned that he could straighten a woman's nose or remove a man's facial birthmark, but the brain was still thinking, "Sick, ugly, unwanted, unacceptable."

It is so easy to believe that life cannot be better, must be tolerated and endured as it is. Jesus was sent to give a new look at your life.

Early one morning my phone rang. An excited voice poured out, "Dr. Biggs, you must help me. I realize the hour is early, but you must help me!" I waited for her to get to the point.

She finally did, "He left. He just packed his bags and walked out."

"Your husband? Are you talking about your husband?"

"Yes, you know Bill."

I asked, "What happened? What kind of argument did you have last night?"

"That's the biggest problem," she said. "There was no argument. There was no fight. He's never done this before. Help me,. Dr. Biggs. Help me get him home again."

"Do you know where he is?"

"Not exactly, but he will be at work in a few minutes. He never misses work. Will you talk to him?"

I asked her to have him call me if he wanted to talk. She agreed to contact him as soon as possible.

His voice was much calmer than hers, "My wife called and said you would like to see me."

"Well, that is not exactly right, Bill. She wants us to get together, you and me."

Within the hour he came into my office and sat down, "Now, Mouzon, let's get the ground rules clear. I am here because my wife wanted me to come, but I do not intend to go home, not today nor tomorrow nor next year."

"What happened to you, Bill? What happened last night?" I asked.

"Oh, it wasn't last night, or the night before. There is no other woman either. Let me say it to you as plain as possible. My wife and I got married twenty-three years ago. The first three weeks of our marriage were fine, very fine. Then one evening I fussed at her because she was not keeping the budget we had prepared together. It was a minor disagreement, but she stormed into the bedroom and started packing her bags. I begged her to sit down and talk. She refused. I asked again; she turned away. Finally, I got down on my knees and begged her to stay."

There was a long pause, a faraway look in his eyes, almost a smile as he remembered better days. Then he said emphatically, "I have been on my knees for twenty-three years, and that's long enough."

When I moved from Houston two years later, their divorce was final. Their marriage had been sick so long; they could not see a possibility for change. But I remember how Jesus healed a man who had been sick even longer than twenty-three years. His first question is so important, "Do you want to be healed?"

"Let Me Do It Now"

Mark 1:14-20
"And at once they left their nets and followed him."
(v. 18 NEB)

The phone rang in my motel room in a Rio Grande Valley town. I had gone there for a three-day preaching mission at the First Methodist Church. The caller identified himself and invited me to join him and the local pastor for lunch that day.

"I guess you think I am awfully pushy just to call and invite you for lunch," he said, "but I'll explain when we pick you up."

After we had ordered our lunch, he continued his explanation. "I have heard you preach five times in this series, and I know that your plane leaves tonight after church. If I was going to talk with you personally, it had to be now."

He then told me that he had been a public school teacher for more than twenty years. But prior to his fiftieth birthday he had had a severe heart attack. During the long weeks of rest and medication, he had tried to develop a positive attitude about his future.

He admitted having a crippling fear at first. Whenever he lifted one foot off the bed, he feared a second attack might take his life.

After days of living with that fear, my host said he came to a new decision. "I am a man with a real faith. My doctors are most capable, my wife and daughter love me, and I refuse to let fear ruin the rest of my life."

He explained how he resolved to follow his doctors' instructions, eat properly, begin simple exercises. His fourth resolution was his most important. "If I hear, read, or have an idea that sounds good, I will act on it as soon as possible. No more delays. If it sounds good for me or others, let me do it now."

With that explanation out of the way, he began to ask me questions. Where was my home? Did I have a wife? Children? How old? How many members in my church? How many attend? Where was I born? Parents still alive? Brothers and sisters? Where does my brother live? My sister? My goals? The things I enjoy most about being a minister? The things that frustrate me most?

Finally, he apologized, "I hope you do not feel that I am a prosecuting attorney. I just felt that you were a new, refreshing voice in our community, and I wanted to know more about you. Thank you for having lunch

139

with me and my pastor. It has meant a lot to me."

As we left the restaurant and he drove away, the pastor said, "He is no fake. He is for real, a marvelous force in our city. This morning at the church breakfast, you mentioned something in your sermon about working harder at one's marriage. You suggested doing special things for the one you love most. His wife was at home with the flu. He stopped on the way home and bought one long-stem red rose with a ribbon on it. He took it to his wife, kissed her on the forehead, and went to work. When I called her later to see how she was feeling, she was still crying quietly about her super terrific husband's thoughtfulness."

That evening as I flew home, I resolved, "If I hear, read, or have an idea that sounds good, I will act on it as soon as possible. No more delays. If it sounds good for me or others, let me do it now."

A Turn at Being Captain

Mark 4:35-41
*"Who can this be? Even the wind and the sea obey
him." (v. 41 NEB)*

He has been hospitalized for seven weeks. The first three weeks he was too sick to do much talking. But then he started feeling better. He is a storyteller of the first rank. The nuns, his friends, and I enjoy nothing more than hearing him talk about his years at sea. He put in more than fifty years on the high seas. Since his early teens he has circled the earth several times as a working seaman and captain.

"Captain Ellis, in all of those years you must have been through some very bad weather," I ventured one afternoon at the hospital. "The thought of rough seas and winds would keep me off ships forever."

"You know, I remember my first bad storm in mid-Atlantic. That was years before hurricanes and storms were tracked so accurately," he recalled. "I was so young. The captain of our ship was an old man to me. He explained how essential it is to maintain a proper attitude of the bow into the wind. If the ship is allowed to drift more than five degrees to port or starboard, it could break apart in high seas."

My mind recalled pictures of Captain Ahab, salt spray in his face.

He continued, "The captain stood on the bridge, his body straight and strong, giving firm command. I went below, climbed in my bunk and went to sleep. During the night thunder and lightning woke me a couple of times, but I slept again. I knew the old man was standing beside the wheel, his face into the storm."

He paused a moment, his eyes far away. Then he began again, "I had a dream that my day would come to be captain of a ship. Months turned to years before my dream came true. I gave the orders, and my ship pulled away from the pier. It was my turn to be captain. I was enjoying my work until one night we met a storm in the Atlantic. And you know what happened?"

I shook my head.

"My men went below and went to sleep. I stood beside the wheel, knowing the weight of responsibility, the loneliness of the night and the storm. Those men had a childlike faith in me. I would not disappoint them. My ship did not drift from its course. I stood there all night, testing the waves and wind, giving my orders to the men on duty. I would not fail them. It was my turn to be captain."

He paused again, took a deep breath, and said, "Mouzon, I was lonely in my responsibility, but not afraid. I know who rules the seas and the men who sail. I know how to live, and I know how to die."